AFRICAN AMERICANS
WHO MADE A DIFFERENCE
15 PLAYS FOR THE CLASSROOM

SCHOLASTIC
PROFESSIONAL BOOKS

New York ◆ Toronto ◆ London ◆ Auckland ◆ Sydney

Thanks to all the talented playwrights who contributed to this collection, and helped to share the stories of these remarkable Americans.

—THE EDITORS

Plays may be reproduced for school-related use. No other part of this publication may be reproduced in whole or in part, or stored in a retrieval system, or transmitted in any form or by any means, electronic, mechanical, photo-copying, recording, or otherwise, without permission of the publisher. For information regarding permission, write to Scholastic Professional Books, 555 Broadway, New York, NY 10012.

Cover and interior design by Liza Charlesworth and Jaime Lucero for Grafica, Inc.

Photo research by Cheryl Moch

Photo credits: Alvin Ailey, Jr.: © The Alvin Ailey American Dance Theater; Romare Bearden: © Adger W. Cowans; George Washington Carver: © Archive Photos; Shirley Chisholm: © Moorland-Spingarn Research Center; Frederick Douglass: © The Schlesinger Library, Radcliff College; Langston Hughes: © Archive Photos; Martin Luther King, Jr.: © United Press International; Thurgood Marshall: © Wide World Photos; Rosa Parks: © AP/Wide World Photos; Jackie Robinson: © AP/ Wide World Photos; Sojourner Truth: © Smith College Collection; Harriet Tubman: © The Library of Congress; Ida. B. Wells-Barnett: © University of Chicago Special Collection; Phillis Wheatley: © Archive Photos; Malcolm X: © UP/Bettmann.

ISBN: 0-590-53546-3

CONTENTS

INTRODUCTION

Welcome to the drama and diversity of *African Americans Who Made a Difference*. These easy-to-read classroom plays provide an intimate look at 15 inspiring men and women, in vocations ranging from politics to painting, civil rights to dance. The plays that follow will enable your students to bear witness to the struggle, pain, grace, and ultimate triumph of these great achievers:

- Alvin Ailey, Jr.
- Romare Bearden
- George Washington Carver
- Shirley Chisholm
- Frederick Douglass
- Langston Hughes
- Martin Luther King, Jr.
- Thurgood Marshall
- Rosa Parks
- Jackie Robinson
- Sojourner Truth
- Harriet Tubman
- Ida B. Wells-Barnett
- Phillis Wheatley
- Malcolm X

If there are two main themes running through the lives of these individuals, they are an iron will and a generosity of spirit. Harriet Tubman escaped the oppression of slavery, then dedicated her life to helping other black men and women do the same. Alvin Ailey, Jr. fought deep prejudice in the conservative dance community, and later went on to found his own company showcasing the talent of fellow African Americans. Baseball great Jackie Robinson withstood the slurs of angry fans and fellow players, to forever dismantle the color barrier in professional sports. And Rosa Parks refused to budge from a bus in Birmingham, Alabama; thereafter ensuring that others would be not be denied the fundamental human right to sit anywhere, undisturbed.

Yes, these are remarkable people. But let's not forget that their histories represent but a few drops in the deep well of black experience. The African-American community, in excess of 22 million, is no-doubt filled with a myriad of unsung heroes—men and women whose lives would certainly qualify for dramatic chronicle and celebration, if we only knew *their* stories.

ABOUT THIS BOOK

The focus of this collection is to broaden student awareness of the important role of African Americans in United States history. Feel free to tailor the presentation of these plays to fit your own classroom needs. For example, some students may enjoy acting in, or producing, the plays for the entire school; while others may feel more comfortable simply reading aloud their parts in a casual readers' theater presentation. The choice is yours . . . and theirs. The important thing is for all kids to participate and learn.

USING THE TEACHER'S GUIDE

Each play includes a complete Teacher's Guide; this section opens with a few select quotes by the featured African American. A mini-biography follows; it provides added information about the individual's life to share with students either before or after the play is presented. Read All About Him/Her is a bibliography containing age-appropriate, easy-to-find titles that will enable children to learn more about these remarkable men and women. The guide culminates in a group of activities designed to strengthen students' thinking, oral, writing, and research skills. Whenever possible, encourage students to work cooperatively on these projects, and to share their work with the rest of the class.

PUTTING ON THE PLAYS

These 15 plays have been designed to enrich your existing curriculum by making social studies come to life in your classroom. The readers' theater format will also bolster your language-arts program because reading plays aloud builds essential oral literacy and reading skills. As you go through the school year and your students become familiar with the format of the plays, you may find that they want to put on more elaborate productions involving props, scenery, costumes, lighting, promotion, tickets—and audiences! Your students may even want to tinker with a play's content by editing or adding new scenes— that's great! Encouraging kids to make these plays their own will only enhance their learning experience.

ALVIN AILEY, JR.
Dancer Extraordinaire

By Harriette Arrington

CHARACTERS (in order of appearance):

INTERVIEWER

ALVIN AILEY: as an adult

ALVIN AILEY: at age 5

ALVIN AILEY: at 9

ALVIN AILEY: at 16

SONNY BOY WILLIAMSON: Blues musician

DANCER

MANUEL: Nine-year-old boy who's Alvin Ailey's friend in Texas

LUCILLE ELLIS: Lead dancer with the Katherine Dunham Company

CARMEN DE LAVALLADE: Alvin Ailey's first dance partner

LESTER HORTON: Founder of his own dance company

DANCER

BROADWAY CHOREOGRAPHER

ACT 1: TEXAS

INTERVIEWER: Mr. Ailey, tell me about growing up in Texas.

ALVIN *(as an adult)*: When I was four or five, I used to work in the cotton fields alongside my mother. On Saturday nights, almost all the adults would go to the Dew Drop Inn to listen to music and dance. I'd sneak out of my house and go stand outside the club. I'd peek through the door and just watch everybody dancing. Sometimes, blues musicians like Sonny Boy Williamson and Blind Lemon Jefferson played at the club.

SCENE 1: 1935. Outside the Dew Drop Inn in Cameron, Texas.

SONNY BOY: *(from inside the club)* I've got to take a short break, but I'll be back. Y'all keep on dancing.

DANCER: *(from inside the club)* One more song, Sonny Boy—come on—just one more song!

SONNY BOY: *(walking out the club's door)* I'll be back. I'll be back. Don't stop dancing.

(Alvin hides under the back porch steps. Sonny Boy pretends not to see him.)

SONNY BOY: I bet there's snakes under this old back porch. I hate snakes. They're mean and nasty, and they hate little boys.

ALVIN *(age 5)*: Snakes like me all right.

SONNY BOY: Is that so? I thought you were out here trying to kick those snakes away from you.

ALVIN *(age 5)*: *(from under the stairs)* I was *dancing*. You play pretty good.

SONNY BOY: You think so? You know an awful lot for a—what are you, about six years old?

ALVIN *(age 5)*: No, sir, I'm five years old.

SONNY BOY: Where's your mama?

ALVIN (*age 5*): She's at home, probably asleep.

SONNY BOY: Where you should be, doing the same thing yourself. What if she woke up and found you gone? She'd be worried sick.

ALVIN (*age 5*): She'd probably figure out where I was. It's not a very big town.

SONNY BOY: Why don't you at least come on out from under that porch?

ALVIN (*age 5*): I will if you play me a song.

SONNY BOY: I will if you dance to it.

SCENE 2: 1939. Beside train tracks outside Cameron, Texas.

MANUEL: I bet the next train's going to be the Sunset Limited. New Orleans to Los Angeles. I'd like to hop on that train and visit *mi abuela* in Los Angeles.

ALVIN (*age 9*): *Abuela, abuela*—don't tell me what it means. Let me guess. *Abuela* means aunt.

MANUEL: Wrong.

ALVIN (*age 9*): Grandmother! Your grandmother lives in Los Angeles.

MANUEL: Yeah. Hey, you're getting pretty good at Spanish.

ALVIN (*age 9*): Man, I wish I lived in Los Angeles. There's nothing to do in this town but watch the trains go by. I wish one of them would stop. I'd hop right on it. Zoom! I'd be long gone!

MANUEL: I think I'm stuck here. I don't think we'll ever move. When I'm a hundred years old, I'll be sitting out here waiting for the next train to go by.

ACT 2: LOS ANGELES

INTERVIEWER: As it turned out, you *did* move to Los Angeles. What happened there?

ALVIN (*as an adult*): My mother Lula Elizabeth and I moved there during World War II. She got a job working in an aircraft factory. Most of the men had quit to

fight in the war. She was one of the first women workers hired. She was one of the first "Rosie the Riveters."

INTERVIEWER: When did you really become serious about dancing?

ALVIN: In high school. I always liked school. I liked learning foreign languages, and I loved reading. Sports—well, that was something else. Gym teacher made me right tackle on the football team. I lasted about two weeks. Then he put me on the track team. I lasted about ten days. Then he made me do gymnastics. I lasted. It was a lot like dancing, and I loved to dance. But I didn't think an African American man had a chance as a dancer—until one day I went by the Biltmore Theater.

SCENE 1: 1940s. Outside the Biltmore Theater in downtown Los Angeles.

LUCILLE ELLIS: *(coming out of stage door)* Child, what are you doing out here? Didn't I see you out here yesterday? And the day before that?

ALVIN *(age 16)*: I've been out here every day.

LUCILLE ELLIS: Have you seen the show?

ALVIN *(age 16)*: Only one time. That's all I could afford. You were great!

LUCILLE ELLIS: Well, what else did you think of it?

ALVIN *(age 16)*: Black guys *dancing* on stage! I've never seen moves like that! And the music—a whole orchestra!—but then, for some dances, there were just a couple of guys playing back-home Texas music. And the costumes!

LUCILLE ELLIS: I think you need to see the show again. You might have missed something. Come on with me. I'll introduce you to the man in charge of the door. He'll let you in free when there's an empty seat.

ALVIN *(age 16)*: You'd do that for me? Why?

LUCILLE ELLIS: Don't ask me why, but I just have this feeling about you.

SCENE 2: 1940s. Jefferson High School gym.

INTERVIEWER: When did you meet Carmen de Lavallade?

ALVIN *(as an adult)*: The first time I saw Carmen de Lavallade was when she was dancing at a school assembly. I'd never seen anything like it. We soon became good friends. She was my first and my best dance partner. I couldn't have made it as a dancer without Carmen.

CARMEN: You shouldn't spend all this time doing gymnastics. You should be dancing.

ALVIN *(age 16)*: And have everybody say I'm a sissy? No, thank you. If I dance, I dance in my room where nobody can see me.

CARMEN: Nobody thinks Lester Horton's a sissy.

ALVIN *(age 16)*: I don't know anybody named Lester Horton. How do I know if he's a sissy or not?

CARMEN: He has a dance studio way out in Hollywood. Come with me to my dance class. I dare you. You can see for yourself what it takes for a man to be a dancer. A sissy wouldn't last for ten minutes at Lester Horton's.

ALVIN *(age 16)*: *(trying to sound casual)* So, you think I could make it as a dancer?

CARMEN: Come with me to Lester Horton's, and find out for yourself.

SCENE 3: A month later. At Lester Horton's Dance Studio in Hollywood.

INTERVIEWER: What did you learn from Lester Horton?

ALVIN *(as an adult)*: Lester? What can I say about Lester? Most dance classes use pianos, but Lester had drums—all sizes and shapes. That first class I went to, the dancers were falling on the floor, and jumping into the air, and doing these strange and weird turns. I wanted to be out there on the dance floor, too. I signed up for classes and found out what it took to be a dancer.

LESTER HORTON: I want you to rehearse with Carmen.

ALVIN *(age 16)*: For what?

LESTER HORTON: Just do it.

ALVIN *(age 16)*: *(walking up to Carmen)* Lester says he wants me to rehearse with you.

CARMEN: Good. Let's get going.

ALVIN *(age 16)*: Just give me five minutes. That last routine wore me out.

CARMEN: *(teasing Alvin)* That last routine? The one I just finished doing? This is a dance class, not gymnastics. There's no room for sissies here.

LESTER HORTON: Ailey! Don't you hear those drums? Dance with Carmen! Now!

ACT 3: NEW YORK

INTERVIEWER: You moved to New York City in the 1950s. What was the dance world like?

ALVIN *(as an adult)*: At that time, some people believed that black dancers didn't belong in ballet. They said that since it had started in Europe, all ballet dancers should be white. Times were tough. I remember trying out for a part in a Broadway musical that was set in Texas. That's me! I thought. Carmen and I went to try out.

SCENE: 1958. Dance studio in Manhattan.

BROADWAY CHOREOGRAPHER: Okay, we've got a musical here called *Ninety Degrees in the Shade*. It's set in Texas.

ALVIN *(as an adult)*: Ninety degrees in the shade—that's Texas, all right.

BROADWAY CHOREOGRAPHER: All you dancers get up here. Show me what you can do. Move, move, move!

ALVIN *(as an adult)*: *(to Carmen)* That choreographer's got to slow down if she wants to get Texas right.

CARMEN: This may be your big chance. Slip in some of your own steps.

BROADWAY CHOREOGRAPHER: *(coming up to Alvin and Carmen)* Wait, wait, wait. You two won't do.

ALVIN *(as an adult)*: But you haven't even seen us dance.

BROADWAY CHOREOGRAPHER: Don't need to. They should have told you. Black dancers won't work in this musical. It's set in Texas. It's set in the past. We can't mix up white and black dancers on stage. That wouldn't have happened. It would be historically incorrect.

ALVIN *(as an adult)*: Historically incorrect? I was born and reared in Texas. What does that make me—historically wrong?

BROADWAY CHOREOGRAPHER: No, no, no. You know what I mean. This musical's about a certain place and a certain time. I can't change that. Listen, better luck next time, okay? Okay?

ALVIN *(as an adult)*: It's a play. It's made up. You can do anything you want to with it.

BROADWAY CHOREOGRAPHER: *(running across the room)* No, no, no! That's the wrong music!

CARMEN: That was the fastest audition I've ever had.

ALVIN *(as an adult)*: Look at those steps. Boring, boring, boring. The music's got nothing to do with Texas. I know what I'd do. No—not what I *would* do— what I *will* do. I'm going to dance my own dances. I'm going to start my own company. It's going to be a place where skin color doesn't matter. Only the way a person moves will matter.

CARMEN: When can I audition?

ALVIN *(as an adult)*: Are you kidding? You already have.

THE END

Teacher's Guide
ALVIN AILEY

QUOTES

I am part of Isadora Duncan. I am part of Martha Graham. I am part of Doris Humphrey. I am part of Asadata Dafora. And I am part of Lester Horton, who made a boy, an eighteen-year-old athlete in sweat pants, feel important.

Dancing hurts . . . You don't make much money. You have to be obsessed with dance to do dance; it's not something you play with.

BIOGRAPHY

Alvin Ailey, Jr., was born in Rogers, Texas, on January 5, 1931. He and his mother, Lula Elizabeth Cooper, lived in a variety of small Texas towns before moving to Los Angeles in 1942. While attending high school, Ailey met a young dancer named Carmen de Lavallade. He accompanied Carmen to Lester Horton's acclaimed Dance Theater School and soon began taking classes there himself. After graduating from high school, Ailey took a clerical job at the Atomic Energy Commission so he could save money for college—and pay for lessons at Lester Horton's. When Horton died suddenly, Ailey took over as choreographer and tried to keep the dance company going. Then Carmen and he were offered jobs as dancers in a Broadway musical called *House of Flowers* and decided to move to New York City.

In 1958, Ailey established the Alvin Ailey American Dance Theater. Still in existence today, the company has a unique style, an energy, and rhythm that's mesmerizing. Ailey's company was the first African-American dance company to perform abroad, on a tour of Southeast Asia sponsored by the U.S. State Department in 1962. Later, Ailey integrated his company to continue to break down racial barriers and stereotypes. In 1969, he established a dance school in Brooklyn, New York.

Ailey received many honors during his lifetime. Among them were the United Nations Peace Medal in 1982 and the Scripps Dance Award for lifetime contributions to American Modern Dance in 1987. Alvin Ailey died in New York City on December 1, 1989.

READ ABOUT HIM

♦ *Alvin Ailey, Jr.: A Life in Dance* by Julinda Lewis-Ferguson (Walker and Company, 1994)

♦ *Alvin Ailey* by Andrea and Brian Pinkney (Hyperion Books for Children, 1993)

♦ *Alvin Ailey* by Kathilyn S. Probosz (Bantam, 1991)

TALK ABOUT HIM

Gotta Dance!: One of the things good dancers do is make their dancing look easy and effortless. Long hours of practice go into a single performance. Ask students about the different forms of dance they've seen—ballet, modern, tap, jazz, hip-hop, and so on. Then discuss what they think the life of a dancer is like. What physical and mental characteristics go into making a good dancer? Encourage students to compare and contrast the life of a dancer to that of an athlete.

Express Yourself: Alvin Ailey's first attempt at choreography was with his dance partner Marguerite Angelos. Ailey said Angelos "could do the most extra-ordinary moves." Today, we know Marguerite Angelos as the poet Maya Angelou. Alvin Ailey, too, loved literature and languages. What do poetry and dance have in common? Make a list of all the different artistic ways that students can think of to express themselves. Which do they find most satisfying, and why?

WRITE ABOUT HIM

A Story in My Life: Many of Alvin Ailey's strongest dances came from childhood experiences in Texas. Ask students to select memorable events or vivid images in their own lives and to write a description of the events. They may also choose to write about current or historical events that have touched them. How would they turn the event into a dance? Depending on their interests, some students may focus on the staging—costumes, sets, music, words—rather than the actual steps.

Rosie the Riveter: Lula Elizabeth Cooper, Ailey's mother, was one of the first women to be employed in the aircraft industry during World War II. Assign students the task of finding out more about "Rosie the Riveter." Suggest that they obtain information from library sources and also by interviewing older family members—such as grandparents or great-aunts and uncles—or family friends who lived during that time period. They might discover that there's a "Rosie the Riveter" in their own family!

ROMARE BEARDEN
An Artist's Life for Him
By Carol Pugliano and Julianna Dunham

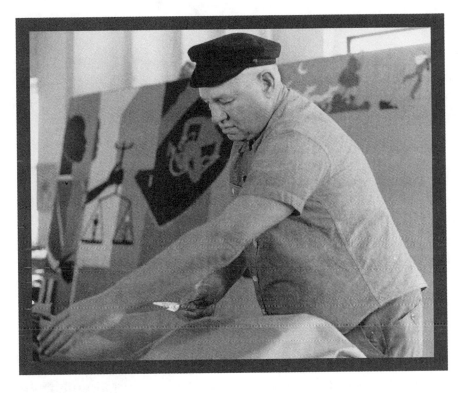

CHARACTERS (in order of appearance):

TOUR GUIDE
TONYA: Student visiting museum
JASON: Student visiting museum
BRYNNE: Student visiting museum
TYLER: Student visiting museum
HALE WOODRUFF: Artist
ERNEST CRICHLOW: Artist and cofounder of Cinque Gallery
NORMAN LEWIS: Artist and cofounder of Cinque Gallery
ROMARE BEARDEN
TEACHER
STUDENTS 1-3

ACT 1

SCENE 1: Present. An art gallery.

TOUR GUIDE: And here we have a Romare Bearden.

TONYA: It's beautiful!

JASON: He's my favorite artist. I mean, just look at what the man did.

BRYNNE: But *how* did he do it? How did he turn his ideas into art like this?

TYLER: Who'd you say did this?

TOUR GUIDE: Romare Bearden. R-O-M-A ...

TYLER: That's okay. You don't have to spell it. Never heard of him.

TONYA: That's the thing. Lots of people have never heard of Romare Bearden.

JASON: Yeah. Even though he's one of the most famous African-American artists around. He's not even mentioned in a lot of art-history books. A lot of African-American artists aren't.

TOUR GUIDE: *(clearing throat)* Romare Bearden was a great collagist.

TYLER: A fine what? You mean like an acrobat or something?

TOUR GUIDE: *(sighing)* Collagist. Someone who works in collage. C-O-L ...

TYLER: Maybe you could *explain* what collage is before you spell it.

TONYA: Collage comes from the French word that means *to put together*.

TYLER: Yeah? I think I remember doing something like that in school. Isn't that where you paste a bunch of pictures all over and on top of each other?

JASON: Sort of. Bearden used photographs and pictures from magazines. Sometimes, he used colored paper and paper he'd painted himself.

BRYNNE: His collages told a lot about African-American culture.

TONYA: But he also believed that his work described all of America, not just black America.

TYLER: *(reaching out to touch the painting)* Some of these things look like they're jumping out at you!

TOUR GUIDE: Don't touch the Bearden! *(clearing throat)* May I continue? *(The others nod.)* Thank you. Romare Bearden became famous for his work in collage, but he started out as a traditional painter. He tried many different types of art until he finally found the one that worked best for him: collage!

TYLER: But what made him choose this kind of art?

TOUR GUIDE: It all started in the 1960s. The civil-rights movement was growing. Romare and his artist friends wanted to get more involved.

SCENE 2: 1963. Bearden's studio in New York City.

WOODRUFF: The times are changing. It's time for black people to come together, to speak out.

CRICHLOW: It's been a long time. We have a lot to say.

LEWIS: We should be working together for change. How can we do that as artists?

BEARDEN: How about working on a group project?

CRICHLOW: I'd love to...but how's that going to help the civil-rights movement?

BEARDEN: It's time for us to come together. With a group project, we can show that we're all working together for the same cause.

WOODRUFF: It would be some project—we all have such different styles.

BEARDEN: We could try collage—the more layers, the better! We'll choose images that express our cause, paste them all together, and paint around them. That way, no one person's style can wipe out anybody else's.

LEWIS: That sounds good, but art's a personal thing, Romie. Maybe I'm selfish, but I just want to do my own thing. Besides, if we're all lumped together, people won't see us as individuals. We won't be taken seriously. What do you think, Hale?

HALE: I like the collage idea, but Norm's got a point. We need to stick together, but we've got to stand out on our own, too.

CRICHLOW: I don't know. Maybe it would be better to keep the art separate. The important thing is that we all believe in the same goal.

SCENE 3: Present. The art gallery.

TOUR GUIDE: Bearden remained interested in collage. He created a few pieces on his own. When an art dealer came to Bearden's studio, he saw the collages and loved them! The dealer promised to show the collages in his next show.

TONYA: Hey, didn't Bearden start his own art gallery in New York City? Is it still around today?

TOUR GUIDE: Indeed it is. Bearden set up the Cinque Gallery with his friends Norman Lewis and Ernest Crichlow. They wanted to have a place where young African-American artists could show their own work. Romare Bearden was very fond of young people. He always visited schools to talk with children.

SCENE 4: A classroom, in 1980.

TEACHER: Students, it gives me great pleasure to present Mr. Romare Bearden!

(The students clap.)

BEARDEN: Thank you very much. I'm very happy to be here. I understand you've been learning about African-American artists.

STUDENT 1: We've learned about Horace Pippin, Jacob Lawrence, and a whole bunch of others.

BEARDEN: It's important to know that there *are* a whole bunch. African Americans have always made great contributions to American art. It's important that we study them and learn what they were all about.

STUDENT 2: Why? Isn't what's happening *now* more important?

BEARDEN: These artists don't live only in the past. You see, each of them had a beginning but no real end.

STUDENT 1: Huh?

BEARDEN: Each of them made a contribution to the painters that followed them. Who knows? Maybe you'll carry on the tradition, too.

STUDENT 2: Where do you get your ideas for your collages?

BEARDEN: Some of the best ideas can come from looking right out your own window. I didn't have to look much farther than outside my studio window, which is right above the Apollo Theater in Harlem.

STUDENT 3: So I could just paint what's right outside my classroom?

BEARDEN: That's right. Start by painting what you know about. You're the expert on your life. And all painting is a kind of talking about life.

SCENE 5: Present. The art gallery.

TYLER: What a cool guy!

TOUR GUIDE: Yes. He was very generous. In fact, before he died, he set up a fund called the Romare Bearden Foundation to help train and educate aspiring young artists. And now, if you'll follow me, we have many more works to see.

(All follow except for Tyler.)

TOUR GUIDE: Won't you be joining us, young man?

TYLER: I'll catch up with you. I just want to hang out here for a little while.

TOUR GUIDE: Very well. Come along, group.

(They exit. Tyler leans toward the painting, about to touch it.)

TOUR GUIDE: *(off stage)* Don't touch the Bearden!

TYLER: *(sighing)* I bet Mr. Bearden would say it's okay to touch it.

THE END

ROMARE BEARDEN

QUOTES

My roots are in North Carolina. I paint what people did when I was a little boy, like the way they got up in the morning.

If you want to work in an art, it wants to help you. But you must go where it leads. I don't 'do' a collage. I just allow some of the people I know to come into the room.

Every artist must find something to set him free, and something he can set free.

BIOGRAPHY

Romare Bearden was born in 1912 in Charlotte, North Carolina. He graduated from New York University in 1935 with a B.S. degree in mathematics. Bearden originally planned to go to medical school, but after drawing cartoons for various publications while at NYU, he realized that he wanted to pursue art as a career.

In 1936, Bearden joined a group of black artists in Harlem called the 306 Group. While working as a caseworker for the New York City Department of Social Services, he painted part time. Then, after serving in the army, Bearden held his first one-man exhibition in New York in 1945 and became increasingly successful. Bearden married dancer and artist Nanette Rohan in 1954.

In 1963 the civil-rights movement inspired him to form the Spiral Group with other black artists to discuss the role of black art in America. In 1969, Bearden founded the Cinque Gallery in New York City with fellow artists Norman Lewis and Ernest Crichlow. This gallery was, and still is, a place for young African-American artists to exhibit their works.

President Ronald Reagan awarded Bearden the National Medal of Arts in 1987, a year before the artist died. Before his death, he requested that a trust fund be established for The Romare Bearden Foundation "to aid, encourage and foster the education and training of deserving and talented art students."

READ ABOUT HIM

◆ *A History of African-American Artists: From 1792 to the Present* by Romare Bearden and Harry Henderson (Pantheon, 1993)

◆ *Romare Bearden* by Kevin Brown (Chelsea House, 1995)

◆ *Free Within Ourselves: African-American Artists in the Collection of the National Museum of American Art* by Regina A. Perry (Smithsonian Institution, 1992)

TALK ABOUT HIM

It Makes Me Feel: Collect a group of Romare Bearden's work to share with the class (see bibliography above for sources). Hold up one piece at a time or allow students to study the works individually. Then ask them to share their immediate responses to Bearden's art. Which piece do they like best? Why? What does the work tell students about American society?

These Days: Romare Bearden's collages often dealt with social issues and events of his time. Which social issues and/or current events concern your students? As a class, discuss the various issues and events. Then ask your student to work in groups based upon their concerns and collaborate on their own collages. They may collect magazine illustrations, newspapers headlines, fabric, colored paper, and other materials to use. Invite other classes to view an exhibit of the collages. What comments does the work inspire?

WRITE ABOUT HIM

Memory Collages: Many of Bearden's collages were also inspired by events from his childhood. Encourage students to bring in photocopies of childhood and family photos (Bearden used photocopied elements in many of his collages). They can then assemble these with paint, crayons, markers, cloth, and pictures from magazines to portray one particularly meaningful memory. Also ask students to write poems or brief memoirs to accompany their collages.

Writing Sounds: While listening to his friend, the drummer Max Roach, on the radio, Romare Bearden tried to capture the sounds and rhythms of the music in paint. "I just took a brush and painted the sounds." Bring in a variety of music by African-American musicians, ask students to jot down words that describe the sounds. Encourage students who respond to particular musicians to find out more about their lives and work.

GEORGE WASHINGTON CARVER
Learn All You Can
By Jaime A. Lucero

CHARACTERS (in order of appearance):

NARRATORS 1–3

GEORGE WASHINGTON CARVER

AUNT SUSAN CARVER: Adopted George and his brother

UNCLE MOSES CARVER: Adopted George and his brother

JUDGE: Official at county fair

MRS. MITCHELL: A neighbor in Diamond Grove

CROWD 1–5 (nonspeaking roles)

MARIAH WATKINS: Formerly enslaved woman who helps George

FARMERS 1–3

ACT 1

SCENE 1. Spring 1871. Late afternoon near the Carver home in Diamond Grove, Missouri.

NARRATOR 1: George Washington Carver was born during the Civil War. It's believed that he was born in 1864, but nobody knows for sure since the births of enslaved people weren't usually recorded. George was an infant when he and his mother were kidnapped by a group of men. Moses Carver, their "owner," managed to rescue George but not his mother. George's father had died earlier in an accident.

NARRATOR 2: George and his older brother Jim were cared for by the Carvers—they called them Uncle Moses and Aunt Susan. George spent most of his time helping Aunt Susan clean, cook, and tend the garden—which he especially liked. He loved plants so much that at the age of seven he created his own secret garden. Every day, after chores, George would disappear to work in his garden and return home late at night. Uncle Moses and Aunt Susan became suspicious of his behavior during these frequent disappearances.

UNCLE MOSES AND AUNT SUSAN: George! George!

GEORGE: Here I am! Over here!

AUNT SUSAN: *(Moving toward George)* Didn't you hear us? We've been hollering your name.

GEORGE: I guess I was so busy working on my garden that I didn't hear you.

AUNT SUSAN: *(looking around in surprise)* You did this all by yourself?

GEORGE: Yes. Do you like it?

UNCLE MOSES: It's beautiful, George.

GEORGE: I learned about growing plants by watching you, Aunt Susan.

AUNT SUSAN: But how in the world did you get them so big and beautiful? My geraniums never looked like these.

GEORGE: By listening to them. The plants tell me what they need.

UNCLE MOSES: *(gently)* Now, son, you know that's foolish. Plants don't talk.

GEORGE: Oh, but they do, Uncle! These plants told me they like it here because they get plenty of sun. Those over there like the shade. That's why they're next to that big tree. And those flowers way over there don't like the cold night air, so at night I cover them, just like I cover myself with a blanket.

UNCLE MOSES: Say, George, think you can help me with my strawberries?

GEORGE: I'd put straw around them if I were you. It'll help keep the ground wet, and you won't have to water them as much.

UNCLE MOSES: Straw? Hmm . . . couldn't hurt to give it a try.

SCENE 2: Summer, 1872. At the Diamond Grove Fair.

JUDGE: Moses Carver, I don't know how you do it, but your strawberries win first prize again! What's your secret?

UNCLE MOSES: Here—*(putting his hands on George's shoulders)*—this is my secret. When it comes to plants, George is a genius!

JUDGE: Him?! But he's just a young boy! He can't be more than seven.

UNCLE MOSES: *(to the crowd)* Go ahead. Ask George anything about plants.

(The people in the crowd whisper to one other; finally, a woman steps out from the crowd.)

MRS. MITCHELL: I have a question. I can't seem to get my petunias to grow. I give them plenty of water, and sun, and you know how rich my soil is. I tell you, George, I'm just about to give up! I don't know what to do.

GEORGE: I think I know what the problem is. It's the soil!

(The crowd roars with laughter.)

JUDGE: Wait, now. Hold on. Give the boy a chance.

(The crowd becomes quiet.)

GEORGE: You see, Mrs. Mitchell, plants are a lot like people. If you eat too much rich food, you're likely to get sick. The same goes for plants.

MRS. MITCHELL: I never thought of that!

JUDGE: *(shaking his head)* He's right. I can't eat more than three pieces of lemon pound cake myself.

GEORGE: I've found that petunias prefer soil mixed with clay.

MRS. MITCHELL: I'm going to run home right this minute and try that!

(The crowd applauds.)

NARRATOR 3: Word about George's talent quickly spread throughout the community. It wasn't long before other neighbors enlisted his help, and he earned the nickname of "The Plant Doctor."

ACT 2

SCENE 1: Several months later at the Carver home. George is about nine years old.

NARRATOR 1: The Carvers wanted to send George to school, but they knew that they couldn't. The nearest school in Diamond Grove was for white children only. Aunt Susan, however, had an idea.

AUNT SUSAN: *(carrying a present)* George, I have a surprise for you.

GEORGE: A surprise? What is it?

AUNT SUSAN: *(handing him the present)* Here.

(George quickly unwraps the gift.)

GEORGE: A book! But, but . . . Aunt Susan, I don't know how to read.

AUNT SUSAN: I know. It's time that you did. Your Uncle and I are going to teach you. That's your real surprise.

GEORGE: You mean just like school?

AUNT SUSAN: Yes, just like school.

SCENE 2: Summer, 1874. The Carver home. George is 12 years old.

NARRATOR 2: Soon, George was reading, writing, and doing mathematics. The years passed, and he learned all that he could from the Carvers. Eager to learn more, George knew it was time to move on.

GEORGE: *(running in, out of breath)* Aunt Susan, Uncle Moses! I just heard about a school I can go to!

UNCLE MOSES AND AUNT SUSAN: Where?

GEORGE: In Neosho!

UNCLE MOSES: Neosho! That's miles away! I'm afraid it's out of the question.

GEORGE: I'll walk every day if I have to. I don't care!

AUNT SUSAN: Your uncle's right. You're only 12 years old, you're way too young to be traveling such a long distance.

UNCLE MOSES: I'm sorry, George.

NARRATOR 3: That night George cried himself to sleep. The next day, he packed some of his belongings and walked the eight miles to Neosho.

SCENE 3: The next morning. A barnyard in Neosho.

NARRATOR 1: Exhausted from his long trip, George found a haystack where he could rest. The haystack was on property belonging to Mariah and Andy Watkins. The Watkins had once been enslaved but were now free.

MARIAH: Who's there?

GEORGE: *(waking up)* It's me, ma'am. George Carver.

MARIAH: Come out to the light where I can look at you. *(looking him over)* Why you're just a young thing! What are you doing here?

GEORGE: *(yawning)* Sleeping, ma'am. I walked all the way from Diamond Grove.

MARIAH: *(surprised)* Diamond Grove! That's a long journey, especially for a child!

GEORGE: I'm going to school. Neosho is the only city around with a black school.

MARIAH: I see. *(thinking)* So, your folks know you're here?

GEORGE: No ma'am. I was planning to write them once I found a place to stay.

MARIAH: So, I suppose you need a place to stay?

GEORGE: Yes ma'am. *(pause)* I won't be much of a bother. You'll hardly know I'm here—plus I can help out with the chores. I can sweep, wash, cook, chop wood, milk the cows, tend the garden ...

MARIAH: *(interrupting)* Whoa, slow down. All right, all right. You can stay here. You won't have to do all those chores, but you can help out with some of them.

GEORGE: Thank you, ma'am. I promise you, you won't regret it.

MARIAH: Here's what I want you to promise me, George Carver: Learn all you can, then go out in the world and give your learning back to our people. Okay? Now, come with me, and I'll get you something to eat. Then we'll write to your folks.

NARRATOR 3: In the days before George started school, Mariah talked about her days as a slave and taught him to read the Bible. She often repeated the promise George had made: Learn all you can, then go out in the world and give your learning back to our people. It was a promise that George Carver kept.

ACT 3

SCENE 1: A farm in Alabama, 1910.

NARRATOR 1: George graduated from Iowa State College in 1896. That same year, he received a letter from Booker T. Washington, asking him to become the head of the Department of Agriculture at Tuskegee Institute, a small school for African-American students in Alabama. George accepted the offer.

NARRATOR 2: Upon arriving at the Institute in September, George discovered that he had little to work with. He quickly rallied his students. Within months,

they created the Institute's first garden, greenhouse, and laboratory! He had so much success in rebuilding Tuskegee, he decided to take his act on the road. The first Movable School of Agriculture was created.

NARRATOR 3: George loaded up a demonstration wagon with all sorts of equipment—a cream separator, a butter churn, steel plows, garden tools, and a cow, for teaching the farmers how to milk! He made it his mission to help rebuild the south after the destruction of the Civil War. Unfortunately, another enemy soon struck the South—the boll weevil—a beetle with long legs and a gray snout.

GEORGE: Good morning, gentlemen. Can I take a moment of your time?

FARMERS 1-3: What?! Who are you?

GEORGE: George Washington Carver, and this is my traveling school.

FARMER 1: You're that plant doctor. You showed Wilson how to fertilize his soil. It did wonders for his cotton crop.

FARMER 2: No, no! He's the one talked that widow into planting peanuts! Peanuts instead of cotton! Who's going to buy peanuts?

FARMER 3: That's crazy! We need practical advice.

GEORGE: If it grows or moos, I can help you with it.

FARMER 1: That so? Take a look at this cotton here. It's got the boll weevil in it. What am I supposed to do now?

FARMER 2: That boll weevil's going to finish off the South.

GEORGE: You need to replace your cotton crops with the peanut crop.

FARMERS 1-3: Peanuts?!

GEORGE: Boll weevil won't touch your peanut crop.

FARMER 2: What can you make out of peanuts? You can't spin them into cloth. How will I sell them?

GEORGE: If you'll come over to my home for dinner tonight, I'll show you.

FARMER 3: You're on!

SCENE 2: Evening of the same day. In George Washington Carver's home.

FARMER 1: Now, Mr. Carver, we're almost done with this delicious dinner, and not once—not once—have you mentioned your beloved peanut.

GEORGE: I'm glad you liked the dinner so much. Everything you just ate contains some form of the peanut.

FARMER 3: What?! You've got to be kidding.

GEORGE: No, I'm not. The milk, greens, and even the chicken sauce! If you'll follow me into the other room, you'll see more products made from the peanut.

(The farmers follow George into the other room.)

FARMER 3: I can't believe my eyes. Oil, paint, ink, rubber ...

FARMER 1: Coffee, candy, vinegar, and lemon drops!

GEORGE: Almost 300 uses in all!

FARMERS 3: You've got to tell someone! Who can you tell?

GEORGE: I'm meeting with Congress next week.

FARMER 1: Congress? That's good.

FARMER 2: Yeah, they'll tell everybody.

FARMER 3: You watch out that those congressmen don't take credit for it!

NARRATOR 3: Carver's meeting with Congress was a huge success. News of his discoveries soon spread worldwide. Thanks to one man, farming was revolutionized. On January 5, 1945, George Washington Carver died, but his legacy lives on.

THE END

GEORGE WASHINGTON CARVER

QUOTES

In all things that are purely social we can be as separate as the fingers, but in all things essential to human progress we are as a single hand.

There are only two ways: One is right and the other is wrong. "About" is always wrong. Don't tell me it's about right. If it's only "about" right, then it's wrong.

BIOGRAPHY

George Washington Carver was born into slavery on a farm in Diamond Grove, Missouri, during the Civil War. It is believed that he was born in about 1864. As an infant George and his mother were kidnapped by Union raiders. Their "owner," Moses Carver, got George back, but George's mother was never found. After the war ended, George became free and remained with the Carvers. Like many formerly enslaved people, he took his owner's last name.

As a boy, George explored the nearby forests and collected rocks and plants. He had a special way with plants. News of his talent spread throughout the community. Neighbors soon brought their sick plants to him and nicknamed him the plant doctor. Mrs. Carver taught George to read at home. When he turned 12, George continued his education at a school eight miles away. He went on to study at Simpson College and then at Iowa State College. There, George became an expert botanist, or plant scientist. In 1896, he accepted a job as a teacher at the Tuskegee Institute in Alabama.

At Tuskegee, George worked hard to teach poor farmers how to improve the soil and grow healthier crops. In 1921, he created 280 products from the peanut and 150 from the sweet potato, including candy, instant coffee, paint, and cereal. Although he remained a teacher at the Tuskegee Institute for the rest of his life, George also became famous throughout the country as an expert on agriculture.

READ ABOUT HIM

* *George Washington Carver: Botanist* by Gene Adair (Chelsea House, 1989)
* *George Washington Carver* by James Marion Gray (Silver Burdett Press, 1991)
* *A Pocketful of Goobers: A Story About George Washington Carver* by Barbara Mitchell (Carolrhoda Books, Inc., 1986)

TALK ABOUT HIM

One Potato, Two Potato: George Washington Carver discovered many uses for the peanut. Another favorite plant of his was the sweet potato, from which he was able to produce more than 150 products including flour, mock coconut, and bread. What other plants can students think of that have numerous uses? Make a list of their suggestions. Which plant or plants is the most versatile?

A Hunger to Learn: As an African-American child, George was barred from attending many schools because they were for white students only. His desire to learn was so strong, however, that he left his home and the only family he'd ever known to attend a school for African-American children. How do your students feel about their own education? Would it seem more precious if schooling were denied them? What if George Washington Carver hadn't been able to go to school? How would our lives today be different because of that?

WRITE ABOUT HIM

A Friendship Between Two Washingtons: Although Carver was dismayed by the meager resources of the Tuskegee Institute, he thought highly of Booker T. Washington, the Institute's founder. Ask students to find out more about the life of Booker T. Washington and/or the Tuskegee Institute.

Southern Landscape: Thomas Edison offered Carver a very good paying job. Carver turned down the inventor because he felt his work was in the South. What were the effects of the Civil War on the southern land? Have students research aspects of southern agriculture, such as King Cotton, boll weevils, a plantation economy, and the number of farms as opposed to factories. What impact did George Washington Carver have on southern agriculture and its economy? Encourage students to show the results of their research in charts and graphs.

SHIRLEY CHISHOLM
Unbought and Unbossed
By Kathleen Conkey

CHARACTERS (in order of appearance):

NARRATORS 1-2

EMMELINE SEALES: Shirley's grandmother

ODESSA: Shirley's sister

MURIEL: Shirley's sister

SHIRLEY CHISHOLM

COLLEGE STUDENTS 1-3

LOUIS WARSOFF: Professor at Brooklyn College

WESLEY HOLDER: Head of Bedford-Stuyvesant Political League

JOHN MCCORMACK: Speaker of the House of Representatives

WILBUR MILLS: U.S. Representative from Arkansas

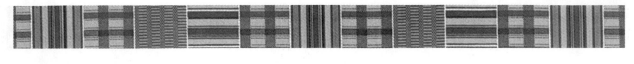

ACT 1

SCENE: 1934. The front porch of Emmeline Seales's house in Barbados. Shirley's grandmother and two sisters sit on the porch.

NARRATOR 1: The year is 1934. A ten-year-old girl, who will one day be known throughout the world as Shirley Chisholm, is preparing to make a long journey from the Caribbean island of Barbados to New York City. Shirley, Odessa, and Muriel St. Hill have lived with their grandmother in Barbados for seven years.

NARRATOR 2: When Shirley was three, her parents, who had immigrated to America, brought the girls to stay with their grandmother in Barbados. At that time, the St. Hills couldn't give their daughters a good home in New York. But Mr. St. Hill had gotten a job at a burlap factory, and his wife worked as a seamstress. Mrs. St. Hill was coming soon to take her daughters back home to New York.

EMMELINE: Shirley, if you don't come out here right this minute, we'll be late! What will your mama think?

ODESSA: Hurry!

SHIRLEY: *(stepping out onto the porch)* I don't want to go to New York City. It's smoky and dirty and noisy and cold. I want to stay here with you, Granny, where it's warm and your cooking is so sweet.

EMMELINE: Your mama and papa have been working their fingers to the bone so they could take you girls home! Now you say you don't want to go?

SHIRLEY: What took them so long?

MURIEL: Yeah, what took them so long?

EMMELINE: Girls, they didn't have a choice. How could they both work so hard and take care of three little girls at the same time? They brought you here because they love you. And it's been my blessing to take care of you.

SHIRLEY: It's not fair that some women can't work and keep their children, too. When I grow up I'm going to be a teacher *and* keep my family right beside me!

EMMELINE: You're a smart girl, Shirley. If you put your mind to something, it gets done. But what you're talking about means changing the whole world.

SHIRLEY: I can do that.

EMMELINE: Oh, child, I believe you just might, but right now we've got to go and meet your mama's boat.

SCENE: 1946. In a classroom at Brooklyn College, Shirley and another student are practicing for a debate.

NARRATOR 1: The year is 1946. Shirley Chisholm is a young woman now. She's about to graduate from Brooklyn College. In high school, Shirley's grades were so high that four colleges offered her scholarships. She chose Brooklyn College so she could stay close to her family.

NARRATOR 2: In college, Shirley studied sociology because she was concerned about relations between blacks and whites and between rich and poor. She also found out that she loved to argue. Shirley was such a persuasive speaker that she was selected to be captain of the College Debating Society.

SHIRLEY: In conclusion, I remind you that all the facts, all the sociological evidence, and indeed, the moral compass inside the heart and soul of each of us, makes clear that every child, whether white or black, rich or poor, deserves a good education and the opportunity to attend college.

(The students and Professor Warsoff applaud.)

STUDENT 1: That was great, Shirley. I'm sure we're going to win.

SHIRLEY: Thank you. It should be a good contest.

(As the students leave, Professor Warsoff approaches Shirley.)

WARSOFF: You're quite a public speaker, Miss St. Hill. Have you thought about what to do when you graduate in June? I hope you've settled on something that will make use of your debating skills.

SHIRLEY: I'm going to teach young children.

WARSOFF: Ah. I'm sure you'll make a fine teacher, but . . . you have so much fire in you—will teaching really hold you attention?

SHIRLEY: Professor Warsoff, surely you agree it's one of the greatest things an adult can do for a child?

WARSOFF: You have me there, Miss St. Hill. Still . . . another great thing you could do is to go into politics. Think of all the people you could help then.

SHIRLEY: Politics?! Professor, how many black women do you know of in politics?

WARSOFF: None, but ...

SHIRLEY: But you think Shirley St. Hill of Brooklyn, New York, can be the first?

WARSOFF: Yes, I do. Why not involve yourself at the local level? Learn the ropes and then run for a local office? Just give it some thought.

ACT 3

SCENE: 1953. Offices of the Bedford-Stuyvesant Political League.

NARRATOR 1: After graduating from Brooklyn College, Shirley taught nursery school during the day. At night, she took classes at Columbia University and received her master's degree in education.

NARRATOR 2: It wasn't long before Shirley was named as director of a day care center. She was in charge of more than 150 children and a staff of teachers and social workers. I almost forgot—she had time to get married to Conrad Chisholm, too! Then something happened that made Shirley Chisholm jump into politics.

SHIRLEY: I'd like to speak to the person in charge, please.

WESLEY: That would be me. I'm Wesley Holder.

(He offers his hand, and the two shake.)

SHIRLEY: I'm Shirley Chisholm. I'd like to do what I can to help Lewis Flagg get elected judge.

WESLEY: We can always use help here at the League. Why don't you tell me a little bit about yourself?

SHIRLEY: I'm the director of the Hamilton-Madison Day Care Center in Manhattan, but I live here in Brooklyn. I've lived here almost all my life. I don't think a lawyer who lives in Manhattan should be elected to be a judge in a community he doesn't know anything about.

WESLEY: The Democratic political bosses here in Brooklyn are the ones who asked the Manhattan lawyer to run here. If you work here for Lewis Flagg, you'll be going against them. They're pretty powerful men.

SHIRLEY: Exactly—that's why I'm here: to help Lewis Flagg get elected.

WESLEY: *(smiling)* When can you start?

SHIRLEY: I already have.

SCENE 1: 1969. The office of John McCormack, Speaker of the House of Representatives in Washington, D.C.

NARRATOR 1: Lewis Flagg was elected. Shirley remained politically active. Professionally, she continued to rise in the ranks. New York City appointed her its chief educational consultant for its day nurseries. In 1964, Shirley ran for the New York State Assembly and won. She was the first African-American woman ever elected to public office in Brooklyn.

NARRATOR 2: Shirley Chisholm continued to add "firsts" to her list. In 1968, she ran and won a place in the U.S. House of Representatives. Her campaign slogan was "Unbought and Unbossed." Soon, Shirley was holding her own against the powerful Democrat who handed out committee assignments to new representatives from his party—the Speaker of the House!

MCCORMACK: I understand that you're upset about the committee you've been put on. Here's the situation: First-year representatives *never* get appointed to the committees they want to be on. Be a good soldier, Mrs. Chisholm.

SHIRLEY: I'm not a soldier, Mr. Speaker. I'm a representative from one of the largest cities in the world, with years of experience inside our schools. Doesn't it make more sense for me to be on the Education Committee, which I asked for, instead of being on the House Agricultural Committee? That's ridiculous! I don't know anything about trees.

MCCORMACK: Then you'll be learning a lot, Mrs. Chisholm. Show your constituents back home what a good learner you are. In a couple of years, we'll see about getting you on the Education Committee.

SHIRLEY: My constituents do not live in rural villages, they live in Brooklyn. There are no forests in Brooklyn. Brooklyn has schools ...

MCCORMACK: Then think of me as your teacher, and do what I tell you to do. Be a good soldier.

SCENE 2: A short time later in a meeting of the House Democrats.

SHIRLEY: Mr. Mills, I want to withdraw my name from the House Agricultural Committee.

MILLS: You can't do that.

SHIRLEY: I will serve the people of my district, and the people of the United States, better on the Education Committee.

MILLS: I'll give you one more chance, Mrs. Chisholm. Will you withdraw your request?

SHIRLEY: *(firmly)* No sir.

NARRATOR 1: Shirley Chisholm and Wilbur Mills stare at each other without saying a word. The other Democrats in the room can't believe what they're seeing and hearing. A week later Shirley is reassigned to the Veterans Affairs Committee. "At least," she said, "there are veterans in Brooklyn. And there is a Veterans Administration Hospital there, too."

NARRATOR 2: After serving in Congress for 14 years, Shirley Chisholm ran for President—the first woman *and* the first African-American ever to run. Although she didn't win the 1972 race, she paved the way for others—Geraldine Ferraro, who ran for vice president in 1984, and Jesse Jackson, who ran for president in 1984 and 1988. More importantly, Shirley Chisholm never let anyone tell her she couldn't achieve exactly what she wanted. She truly was "Unbought and Unbossed."

THE END

Teacher's Guide
SHIRLEY CHISHOLM

QUOTES

Granny gave me strength, dignity, and love. I didn't need the black revolution to teach me that.

I stand before you today as a candidate for the Democratic nomination for the presidency of the United States. I am not the candidate of black America, although I am black and proud. I am not the candidate for the women's movement of this country, although I am a woman, and I am equally proud of that. I am not the candidate of any political bosses or special interests—I am the candidate of the people.

BIOGRAPHY

Shirley Chisholm was born Shirley St. Hill in Brooklyn, New York, in 1924 to parents who had emigrated from the West Indies. After graduating from Brooklyn College in 1946 with a degree in sociology, she attended night school at Columbia University for her master's degree in education. There Shirley met her first husband, Conrad Chisholm, whom she married in 1949. After she and Conrad divorced in 1977, she married architect Arthur Hardwick, Jr. Chisholm's teaching career began at Mt. Calvary Child Care Center in Harlem. In 1953 she was appointed director of Friends' Day Nursery in Brooklyn; in 1959 she joined the New York City Division of Day Care and eventually became chief educational consultant.

Politically active in college, Chisholm went on to participate in politics in her community. In 1953 she became associated with the Bedford-Stuyvesant Political League; in the early '60s she helped form the Unity Democratic Club, an important black political club in Brooklyn. Chisholm ran for State Assembly in 1964, where she served two terms. She won a Congressional seat in 1968 and became the first African-American woman in Congress. While in Congress, she helped found the Congressional Black Caucus. Although she didn't win, Chisholm's historic run for President in 1972 helped galvanize the budding women's movement. After retiring from Congress in 1982, she taught political courses at Mount Holyoke College and became chair of the National Political Caucus of Black Women. Today, Shirley Chisholm remains an active and outspoken supporter of women's and African-American rights.

READ ABOUT HER

- *Famous Firsts of Black Women* by Martha Ward Plowden (Pelican, 1993)
- *Shirley Chisholm* by Jill S. Pollack (Franklin Watts, 1994)
- *Shirley Chisholm: Teacher & Congresswoman* by Catherine Scheader (Enslow, 1990)

TALK ABOUT HER

Authority Figures: Shirley Chisholm was famous for questioning authority. For instance, she once joined in a boycott of President Nixon's State of the Union address after he refused to meet with members of the Congressional Black Caucus. Ask students if they've ever wanted to say "no" to authority figures. Did they do it? If so, what happened? If not, why didn't they? You may wish to share your own experiences as an authority figure that has been challenged.

That's Debatable: Shirley Chisholm loved to debate. In college, she argued such topics as whether or not eighteen-year-olds should be given the right to vote and the pros and cons of capital punishment. Randomly divide the class into two groups, the pros and the cons. Throw out a current topic and let the two groups debate it. Before beginning the debate, each group should meet to discuss its strategy. Afterwards, discuss students' individual feelings about the topic.

WRITE ABOUT HER

Who Speaks for Us?: Shirley Chisholm was the first African-American woman elected to the U.S. Congress. What is the make up by ethnicity and gender of the U.S. Congress today ? How does the class population compare to that of the Senate or House of Representatives? To begin the activity, have students make two circle graphs—one should show the ethnic breakdown of the class and the other should show the breakdown by gender. Then they should create circle graphs that show the ethnicity and gender of the Congress.

A Bill's Own Life: Nine of the bills that Shirley Chisholm introduced to the New York State Assembly passed. Which issues most concern your students? What would they like to see changed in our society? Suggest that students draft bills addressing their concerns. Then they can circulate their bills to their classmates and try to win support. What kinds of compromises are they willing to make to get their bills passed? How do their final versions compare to their first drafts? Students should present the final versions of their bills to the rest of the class for a vote.

FREDERICK DOUGLASS
Reading, Writing, and Freedom

By J. Haakmat

CHARACTERS (in order of appearance):

NARRATOR

FREDERICK DOUGLASS

BETSEY BAILEY: Frederick's grandmother

SALLY: Young enslaved girl on Anthony plantation

AUNT KATY: Enslaved woman on Anthony plantation

SOPHIA AULD: Hugh's Auld's wife

HUGH AULD: Frederick's master in Baltimore

ISAAC ROLLS: A friend of Frederick's

CONDUCTOR

WILLIAM GARRISON: Abolitionist (a person who's against slavery)

WILLIAM C. COFFIN: A friend of Frederick's

ANNA MURRAY DOUGLASS: Frederick's wife

PEOPLE AT ANTISLAVERY RALLY 1-5 (nonspeaking roles)

ACT 1

SCENE 1: A hot summer day, probably 1824. On Edward Lloyd's wheat plantation near Hillsborough, Maryland.

NARRATOR: Until he was six years old, Frederick Douglass lived in a cabin with his cousins, grandparents, and uncle. The cabin was on a wheat plantation owned by a wealthy man named Edward Lloyd. As Frederick soon found out, he and his family "belonged" to the plantation manager: Aaron Anthony.

FREDERICK: I'm tired, Grandma. I want to go home.

BETSEY: You can take two more steps, can't you? See that porch? I want you to wait right there while I go inside.

FREDERICK: I don't want to! Please, let's go back home, Grandma!

BETSEY: *(in a stern voice)* We're slaves, Fred. We're Master Anthony's property. We can't do what we want. *(in a softer voice)* Now please, no more moaning.

FREDERICK: Do we have to stay long? When will we go back home, Grandma!

BETSEY: *(softly)* Fred, I don't have time for this. I've got to go into the house for a bit. You'll feel better if you stop this silliness and go play with Sally.

(Betsey goes into the big house. Frederick wanders over to Sally.)

SALLY: You can stare at the door all you want, but she isn't coming back. She left out the side door and is already on her way back home . . . without you.

FREDERICK: *(shouting)* Grandma! Grandma!

(Aunt Katy steps out of the door of the big house.)

AUNT KATY: Stop your crying, child!

FREDERICK: Where's my Grandma?

AUNT KATY: She's gone. *(in a gentle voice)* Now go on out in the yard.

SALLY: Told you. I know. That's how I lost my mother and my baby brother.

FREDERICK: *(trying to be brave)* They'll be back. You'll see.

SCENE 2: About two years later in Master Anthony's front yard.

NARRATOR: Frederick drove cows, chased hens out of the garden, kept the front yard clean, and ran errands. His meals consisted of mush—boiled corn-meal. His bed was a sack used for carrying corn.

FREDERICK: Aunt Katy, I'm starving. You got anything to spare in the kitchen?

AUNT KATY: You hush up, now. I've got some news. The Master's sending you off to Baltimore, to some of his relations. You'll be taking care of their son.

FREDERICK: I don't want to leave here! What if my grandmother comes back here looking for me? I don't want to take care of nobody's son. Where's my mother? Why isn't she here taking care of me?

AUNT KATY: Hush, now! You'll get us all into trouble, talking like that! You've got no say in the matter. You're leaving first thing tomorrow morning.

FREDERICK: I'll run away!

AUNT KATY: And just where do you think you'd run to, child?

FREDERICK: I'll just run and run till I can't run anymore. That's where I'll go.

AUNT KATY: In deep trouble is where you'll end up. *(whispering)* It won't be so bad, you'll see. I'll pack you a nice lunch, slip in some chicken and cornbread.

FREDERICK: Chicken *and* cornbread? Maybe it won't be so bad.

ACT 2

SCENE 1: A year later. At the home of Hugh and Sophia Auld in Baltimore, Maryland.

NARRATOR: Frederick wasn't sorry to leave the plantation behind. He was sent to the home of Hugh and Sophia Auld, where he took care of their little son, Thomas. At first Sophia Auld was kind to him. She began to teach Frederick the alphabet and how to spell.

SOPHIA AULD: See if you can read these words, Frederick.

FREDERICK: Ant. Pat. Sat. Ask.

SOPHIA AULD: Perfect!

HUGH AULD: *(entering the kitchen.)* I see a book in that boy's hands, but I cannot believe my eyes.

SOPHIA AULD: I've been teaching Frederick to read. We were waiting to surprise you—he's such a smart child.

HUGH AULD: Take the book away, Sophia. There will be no more lessons. Don't look at me like that. I mean it—no more lessons. If you give a slave an inch, he will take a mile. All a slave should know is that he must obey his master.

SOPHIA AULD: I see no harm in teaching Frederick a few words. It will make him more useful...

HUGH AULD: No harm!? It's against the law! Learning spoils the best slaves in the world. If you teach that boy to read, there will be no keeping him!

(The Aulds leave the room. Sophia is carrying the book.)

FREDERICK: *(to himself)* So that's it! Reading is the way to freedom.

NARRATOR: After that, Sophia Auld became hard on Frederick. Nothing, however, could stop him from continuing his education. As he hurried to and from the Auld's house on errands, he met other boys. Some of them were white. At every chance, Frederick made friends and got them to teach him what they knew.

ACT 3

SCENE 1: September 3, 1838. At a train station in Baltimore.

NARRATOR: When "master" Aaron Anthony died suddenly, Frederick was sent back to the plantation. Then he was passed from owner to owner. For a little while, he returned to the Aulds in Baltimore. Soon he was called back to the country and hired out as a field hand. In 1835, Frederick attempted to escape, but was caught and jailed. Fearful that he would stir up trouble, Frederick's owner packed him off to Hugh Auld in Baltimore again. There, Frederick met

and fell in love with Anna Murray, a free black woman. Anna and his friend Isaac Rolls helped Frederick to escape to the North.

ISAAC: Soon as the train's about to pull out, I'll drive by the ticket window real fast. You just hop out of the cab and jump on that train. You sure you got your papers?

FREDERICK: I'm sure. Let's hope the conductor's too busy to take a close look at them. I don't exactly match the description. I'm not a 54-year-old sailor.

ISAAC: No, but you sure look like a *young* sailor. Anna sewed you up a nice sailor suit.

FREDERICK: If it weren't for her, I wouldn't be able to do this.

NARRATOR: Isaac suddenly shook the reins, and the horses galloped forward. The train was starting to leave the station. Frederick barely had time to shake Isaac's hand before he leapt on board the moving train. He found his way to the "colored car" and sat down. The conductor entered the car. He moved slowly and steadily toward Frederick, stopping to examine each person's "free" papers—the papers all free black people had to carry.

CONDUCTOR: *(stopping in front of Frederick)* Papers.

FREDERICK: I never carry my free papers to sea with me. I only carry my seaman's papers. Here they are.

CONDUCTOR: You're supposed to carry your free papers with you all the time. How am I supposed to know whether you're really free or not? It's not like you look different if you're free.

FREDERICK: But I do look like a sailor, right? I'm on my way to the docks. I'm getting ready to ship out.

CONDUCTOR: *(sighing)* All right, all right. Let me take a look at your seaman's papers.

NARRATOR: As Frederick tried to appear confident, the conductor unfolded the papers. Luckily, he didn't read them. He only took a look at the eagle at the top of the page and then returned them to Frederick. After leaving the train, Frederick boarded a ferry that crossed the Susquehanna River. It was a popular ferry. Frederick saw three white men who knew him—men who knew he wasn't

a sailor—and a friend. Luckily, he managed to avoid being recognized. A few days later, Frederick and Anna met in New York City.

SCENE 2: August 16, 1841. An antislavery convention in Nantucket, Massachusetts.

NARRATOR: Frederick and Anna get married and move to New Bedford, Massachusetts. There, they become involved with the abolitionist, or antislavery, movement. A turning point comes in Frederick's life when he attends an antislavery convention with Anna and a white friend, William C. Coffin. William Garrison, a white abolitionist, spoke to the crowd.

GARRISON: And so, my friends, our purpose today is to find more ways to communicate the evils of slavery to our community and the world at large. I would now like to give the podium over to anyone who wishes to speak towards this end.

COFFIN: *(whispering to Frederick)* Tell them your story.

FREDERICK: What would I say? I've never spoken in front of a crowd before. Why would these people want to hear my story?

COFFIN: Look around you, Frederick. None of these white women and men here today have experienced what you have.

ANNA: Think of all the people you can speak for. Think of all those who aren't free to speak for themselves. You're their voice. You *must* tell your story.

GARRISON: Will there be any speakers from our audience?

FREDERICK: *(standing)* Yes, I want to speak. My name is Frederick Douglass. I was born a slave. I was raised by my Grandmother until, at the age of six, a day came that I will never forget—the day I was taken from my family. Life as a slave was difficult. The worst part was thinking there was no way out. But I learned the secret to freedom when I was about twelve. Reading and writing. These tools gave me the strength to escape slavery...and to stand in front of you today. For the rest of my life, I will work to help end slavery. And I invite you to join me in that fight.

(The crowd bursts into applause.)

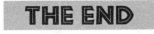
THE END

FREDERICK DOUGLASS

QUOTES

I have no accurate knowledge of my age. By far the larger part of slaves know as little of their ages as horses know their's, and it is the wish of most masters within my knowledge to keep their slaves thus ignorant. I do not remember to have ever met a slave who could tell of his birthday.

The truth was, I felt myself a slave, and the idea of speaking to white people weighed me down. I spoke but a few moments, when I felt a degree of freedom, and said what I desired with considerable ease.

BIOGRAPHY

Frederick Douglass was probably born in 1817 near Hillsborough, Maryland. Like his mother and his grandmother, he was born into slavery. At the age of six, Frederick was separated from his family and taken to live in the plantation house managed by his "owner" Aaron Anthony. Two years later, he was sent to Baltimore to look after the son of Hugh and Sophia Auld. Sophia Auld began to teach Frederick until her husband put a stop to it. Undeterred, Frederick continued his education on the streets by convincing educated white boys to give him lessons.

When Aaron Anthony died, Frederick—legally considered part of Anthony's property—had to return to the plantation. Then he fell under the charge of Anthony's daughter, Lucretia, until she died suddenly. Her husband Thomas, Hugh Auld's brother, let Frederick go back to Baltimore. A fight between the two brothers resulted in Frederick's having to return to the country. Thomas Auld hired Frederick out to other farmers. On one of the farms, he began to teach other slaves to read. In 1835, he tried to escape but was caught and taken to jail. Afraid that Frederick would cause trouble, Thomas Auld sent him back to Baltimore. In 1838, Frederick finally escaped to the North.

In addition to becoming active in the abolitionist movement and writing three autobiographies, Douglass was the publisher and editor of a weekly reform publication called *North Star*. He was appointed as minister-resident and consul-general to Haiti and chargé d'affaires for the Dominican Republic by President Benjamin Harrison. Frederick Douglass died on February 20, 1865.

READ ABOUT HIM

* *The Narrative of the Life of Frederick Douglass: An American Slave* by Frederick Douglass (New American Library, 1968)
* *Escape from Slavery: The Boyhood of Frederick Douglass in His Own Words* edited and illustrated by Michael McCurdy (Alfred A. Knopf, 1994)
* *Frederick Douglass: The Last Day of Slavery* by William Miller (Lee & Low Books, 1995)

TALK ABOUT HIM

Reading Means Freedom: Frederick Douglass was able to find his way to freedom through reading. Discuss with your students the ways in which reading can make a person free. Encourage them to think about the practical aspects—such as understanding warning signs. Also, point out the imaginative benefits of reading.

Body or Mind?: It was illegal for an enslaved person to receive an education. The owners knew that knowledge is power. Ask kids to think about the effects of enslaving people physically by controlling their movements or mentally by controlling their access to information. Is one form worse? Discuss their answers.

WRITE ABOUT HIM

The ABC's of Frederick Douglass: Like all readers, Frederick Douglass started out learning the alphabet. Have students create an alphabet that describes the life of Frederick Douglass. The letter *A*, for instance, could stand for *abolition* or Hugh and Sophia *Auld*. The words can describe ideas, or be real people, places, or events. Encourage students to illustrate the alphabet. You may wish to divide the class into groups. See how many letters each can do.

The Autobiography of Frederick Douglass: Without an education, Frederick Douglass wouldn't have been able to write his autobiography. Enslaved people who didn't have access to an education couldn't write down what happened to them. They relied on other art forms. Read aloud excerpts from Douglass's autobiography to your students. Let groups of students choose other ways to bring his writing to life. They may wish to act out the scene, illustrate or choreograph it, write a poem or song, or retell it as a form of oral history.

The Abolition Movement: Have students find out more about the abolitionist movement in the United States and its leaders. Ask them to use their research to create a report about a leading abolitionist, including graphics (photographs, drawing, timelines, maps, etc.) as well as text (brief biography, interesting facts, quotes, etc.)

LANGSTON HUGHES
Answering the Knock of Opportunity

By Egypt Freeman

CHARACTERS (in order of appearance):

NARRATORS 1-3

CHARLES JOHNSON: Editor of the Urban League's *Opportunity* magazine

MS. JESSIE FAUSET: Editor of *Brownies' Book*

LANGSTON HUGHES

CARL VAN VECHTEN: Writer and critic

BUSBOY

WAITRESS

VACHEL LINDSAY: Poet

ACT 1

SCENE 1: May 1925. At an awards banquet given by *Opportunity* magazine in New York City.

NARRATOR 1: Many African Americans from the South, eager for work (and for what they hoped would be a better life), moved to the North. Many found homes for themselves in places like Harlem in New York City.

NARRATOR 2: In the South, there were many harsh laws that treated blacks unfairly. They couldn't eat in the same restaurants, stay at the same hotels, or even use the same drinking fountains as whites. The laws in the North were less harsh, but living there wasn't always easier for African Americans.

NARRATOR 3: Although many of the African Americans who lived there were poor, Harlem was bustling with creativity. Musician Eubie Blake; painter Romare Bearden; and writers Zora Neale Hurston, Richard Wright, and Langston Hughes all lived there. African Americans often found it difficult to find jobs performing in white-owned jazz clubs, to have their work displayed in white-owned galleries, or to get their writing published in white-owned magazines. In Harlem, however, there were black-owned clubs, galleries, and magazines. At a banquet hosted by *Opportunity* magazine, Langston Hughes would make an important connection that led to a lasting professional relationship—but he had to grab the opportunity!

CHARLES JOHNSON: Langston! Welcome back to New York. I'm so glad you're here.

JESSIE FAUSET: We've missed you! Where have you been?

LANGSTON: Africa, the Netherlands, Paris, Italy—and Jones Point, New York.

CHARLES JOHNSON: Well, I hope you've come back with a suitcase full of new poems.

JESSIE FAUSET: Langston, I don't think you realize it yet, but you're one of the finest black writers we have—in fact, you're one of the finest writers around, black or white or any other color!

LANGSTON: It's hard enough to believe that one of my poems is up for an award here. I keep pinching myself!

CHARLES JOHNSON: Carl Van Vechten's here tonight. He wants to meet you.

LANGSTON: *The* Carl Van Vechten? The writer and critic? That Carl Van Vechten?

CHARLES JOHNSON: Well, he's heard of you, too. In fact, he's quite a fan of yours!

LANGSTON: Carl Van Vechten a fan of mine? You're kidding!

JESSIE FAUSET: Carl Van Vechten is very interested in what's going on up here in Harlem. You're a part of that. It's a rebirth for us and our creativity.

CHARLES JOHNSON: That's right. Van Vechten's always coming up to Harlem to listen to jazz at The Cotton Club. I always see him at the readings our writers give up here.

JESSIE FAUSET: *And* you should see the parties he and his wife give. All *kinds* of artists and writers, black and white, meet there. Critics, agents, and publishers go there, too.

CHARLES JOHNSON: He's been working for a long time to bring our work to a larger audience.

HUGHES: *(Playfully holding his chest, as if in shock)* And you say that Carl Van Vechten wants to meet *me*?

(Van Vechten overhears their conversation. He steps forward, smiling, and holds out his hand to shake Langston's.)

CARL VAN VECHTEN: Yes, I do.

CHARLES JOHNSON: Langston, as you've probably already guessed, this is Carl Van Vechten.

LANGSTON: *(shaking Van Vechten's hand vigorously)* It's a pleasure to meet you, sir!

CARL VAN VECHTEN: The pleasure is all mine, Mr. Hughes. Please, call me Carl.

LANGSTON: Only if you call me Langston.

CARL VAN VECHTEN: It's a deal. I've been looking forward to meeting you for a long time. I read your poem, "The Negro Speaks of Rivers"—and said to myself, "I've got to meet the man who wrote this." I love that poem so—it's like music:

> I've known rivers:
> I've known rivers ancient as the world and older than the flow of
> human blood in human veins.
> My soul has grown deep like the rivers.

LANGSTON:

> I bathed in the Euphrates when dawns were young.
> I built my hut near the Congo and it lulled me to sleep.
> I looked upon the Nile and raised the pyramids above it.
> I heard the singing of the Mississippi when Abe
>   Lincoln went down to New Orleans and I've seen
>   its muddy bosom turn all golden in the sunset.
> I've known rivers:
> Ancient, dusky rivers.
>
> My soul has grown deep like the rivers.

CARL VAN VECHTEN: Yes . . . the rhythm is almost like music!

LANGSTON: *(excitedly)* That's exactly what I'm trying to do, to give my words the feeling of the blues, or those songs you'd hear in southern juke joints, or the nightclubs up in Harlem.

CARL VAN VECHTEN: You've succeeded. Your poems seem to flow like blues songs. I can't tell you how much they've moved me. And what I want to know is this: Have you ever thought of publishing a book of your work?

LANGSTON: *(shaking his head in frustration)* I have—it's the publishers who haven't.

CARL VAN VECHTEN: Maybe you just need a little help from a friend.

LANGSTON: *(laughing)* Sure, as long as that friend owns a publishing company.

CARL VAN VECHTEN *(laughing, too):* You've got *me*, for what that's worth! Look Langston, I'm having lunch with my publisher, Alfred Knopf, and, if it's all right with you, I'd like to let him take a look at some of your poems. I won't do it without your permission.

LANGSTON: That would be a dream come true! But listen—I don't want to make it by asking for special favors. If Alfred Knopf publishes my poetry, I want it to be because he truly believes it's worth publishing.

CARL VAN VECHTEN: Trust me, Langston, Alfred Knopf doesn't publish work he doesn't believe in. I'm glad to have you as a new friend, but that's not why I want to show him your work. I'm doing it because your poetry is brilliant. It deserves a wider audience. Let's get this straight at the beginning. All I'm doing is providing an opportunity—it's up to you to take it!

LANGSTON: Don't worry, Carl. When I hear opportunity knocking, I open the door.

NARRATOR 1: Opportunity was knocking loud and clear. The lunch meeting between Carl Van Vechten and Alfred Knopf went very well. Just 17 days after meeting Van Vechten at the *Opportunity* dinner in New York, Hughes signed a contract with Knopf for the publication of his first book of poems, *The Weary Blues*.

ACT 2

SCENE: Late November 1925. The dining room of the Wardman Park Hotel in Washington, D.C.

NARRATOR 2: Even after signing a publishing contract, Langston was far from rich. Unfortunately, life hadn't changed much at all. He had planned on attending Howard University, but he wasn't able to get a scholarship.

NARRATOR 3: To make ends meet, Langston worked as a busboy at the Wardman Park Hotel. One night, while working there, he made another connection that would help introduce him to the nation as a talented writer.

BUSBOY: Whoa! Don't leave yet, Langston!

LANGSTON: Why? Don't tell me there's another party of 20 sloppy people I have to clean up after!

WAITRESS: *(joking)* Don't worry—it's probably only about 15 sloppy people.

BUSBOY: *(winking at the waitress)* No man, it's worse! Some famous *poet* is coming to read his rhymes at the hotel tonight.

WAITRESS: What's wrong with poets? Langston here writes poems, you know.

BUSBOY: It's just that they're such rotten tippers! *(He laughs.)*

WAITRESS: Oh . . . I get it. Because they're all starving— right?

LANGSTON: That's for sure! *(laughing)* So who's this famous poet that's coming here tonight?

BUSBOY: The manager said his name was . . . Lindsay something.

LANGSTON: Lindsay something? Are you sure it isn't Vachel Lindsay?

BUSBOY: *(snapping his fingers)* Yeah, that's it! Whoever you just said.

LANGSTON: Why didn't you say so? HHHHhhhmmmm . . . this could be a good opportunity for me to meet him!

BUSBOY: How?

WAITRESS: Yeah, how? You can't just walk up to the man while he's eating his dinner and say, "Hi, I'm a poet, too . . . wanna be my friend?"

LANGSTON: Don't worry, I've got a plan.

NARRATOR 1: Langston quickly wrote out three of his poems on pieces of paper and put them in the pocket of his jacket. When Vachel Lindsay came down for dinner, Langston quickly laid the poems beside the poet's plate and walked away. He didn't know what to say to Lindsay.

NARRATOR 2: Later that night, while listening to Lindsay's reading, Langston was surprised to hear the poet talking about *him*.

LINDSAY: The work of a very promising young poet has been brought to my attention, and I'd like to share it with you.

WAITRESS AND BUSBOY: *(grabbing Langston's arm, shaking it up and down, and slapping his back)* Langston, man, that's got to be you he's talking about!

LINDSAY: *(reading from one of the pieces of paper Langston left beside his plate)*
    I, too, sing America.
    I am the darker brother.

They send me
To eat in the kitchen
When company comes,
But I laugh,
And eat well,
And grow strong.
Tomorrow,
I'll be at the table
When company comes.
Nobody'll dare
Say to me,
"Eat in the kitchen,"
Then.

Besides,
They'll see
How beautiful I am
And be ashamed—

I, too, am America.

NARRATOR 3: The next day the members of the press surrounded Langston. They photographed him at the hotel in his busboy's uniform and asked him all about himself.

NARRATOR 1: By the end of the month, the story of how a quiet busboy had been discovered by a famous poet had been carried all over America by the Associated Press wire service. The episode produced all the publicity Langston needed to launch the publication of *The Weary Blues* in January 1926. In addition to being a fine poet, Langston Hughes wasn't afraid to seize opportunity when it presented itself.

THE END

Teacher's Guide

LANGSTON HUGHES

QUOTES

An artist should be free to choose what he does, certainly, but he must also never be afraid to do what he might choose.

We build our temples of tomorrow, strong as we know how, and we stand on top of the mountain, free within ourselves.

BIOGRAPHY

James Langston Hughes was born on February 1, 1902 in Joplin, Missouri. His work as a poet, novelist, and playwright has made him one of the most important writers in America.

After publishing his first poem in a major magazine at the age of 19, Hughes moved to New York City to join the increasing number of African-American artists who flocked to the community of Harlem during the 1920s and 1930s— a time which became known as the Harlem Renaissance. During this period, Hughes created a style of poetry which used the rhythms of jazz and the story-telling of blues to uniquely portray the black experience.

While New York remained an important base throughout his lifetime, he traveled completely around the globe to experience, firsthand, the many cultures of the world. Langston Hughes was an inspiration to many black writers who followed him, and he remained an active contributor to the literary world up until his death in New York City on May 22, 1967.

* *Popo and Fifina* by Arna Bontemps and Langston Hughes (Oxford, 1993)
* *Coming Home: From the Life of Langston Hughes* by Floyd Cooper (Philomel, 1994)
* *The Dreamkeeper and Other Poems* by Langston Hughes (Knopf, 1993)
* *Langston Hughes* by Jack Rummel (Chelsea House, 1988)

TALK ABOUT HIM

Rhythm and Blues: Langston Hughes tried to capture the rhythm of jazz and blues songs in his poetry. His friend, the poet Countee Cullen, used a very different, classical structure. Select poems by each poet and encourage students to discuss the differences in style, rhythm, content, and use of language. You may wish to let volunteers study the poems and then recite them aloud, so students can really "hear" the differences.

Building Bridges or Poems?: James Hughes, Sr., wanted his son Langston to study engineering, as he had. In fact, he agreed to finance Langston's education only if he promised to study engineering. However, after his first year at Columbia University, Langston left because he wanted to have more time to write. His father was very upset, which created problems between them. Ask students why they think Langston's father wanted him to major in something "practical." If students had to choose between doing work that they loved or doing work that paid well, which would they pick?

WRITE ABOUT HIM

The Harlem Renaissance: The 1920s through the 1930s was a period when black artists and writers were gaining increasing recognition for their talents and contributions to American culture. Since Harlem was the center of much creative activity, this period became known as the Harlem Renaissance. Have students research this period, and present reports on other famous black writers, musicians, and artists who gained prominence at this time. Encourage students to use a variety of media in their presentations to the class.

A Renaissance Man: Langston Hughes was an incredible storyteller who used many different forms to express himself: poetry, short stories, plays, and nonfiction. After students have read a variety of Hughes's work, let them select their favorite pieces. They may illustrate them, explain the reasons for their choices, and include a biography of the writer in a class book of Hughes's collected work. To introduce other students to Langston Hughes, share their book with other classes.

MARTIN LUTHER KING, JR.

Nonviolence on the Move

By Frank Caropreso

CHARACTERS (in order of appearance):

NARRATORS 1-3

DR. MARTIN LUTHER KING, JR.

REVEREND RALPH ABERNATHY: Civil rights activist, one of King's best friends

ROSA PARKS: "Mother of the civil rights movement"

WHITE BUS DRIVER

WHITE MALE PASSENGER

CORETTA SCOTT KING: Martin's wife

ROBERT KENNEDY: Attorney General of the U.S. and John's brother

GUARDS 1-2

A. PHILIP RANDOLPH: Labor leader and civil rights activist

CROWD 1-5

ACT 1

SCENE: December 1956. Bus stop in Montgomery, Alabama.

NARRATOR 1: In 1954, Martin Luther King, Jr., became the new pastor at the Dexter Avenue Baptist Church in Montgomery, Alabama. He preached nonviolence as a way to change inequality. Dr. King urged his congregation to fight against segregation by joining the NAACP (the National Association for the Advancement of Colored People), and registering to vote. Then, on December 1, 1955, something happened that changed Martin Luther King, Jr.'s life—and American history.

NARRATOR 2: Rosa Parks refused to give up her seat on a bus to a white person. The African-American community rallied behind her. A boycott was called against the bus company. A committee, the Montgomery Improvement Association (MIA), was formed to lead the boycott. Martin Luther King, Jr. was elected as its president.

NARRATOR 3: Martin was arrested. It was against Alabama state law to take part in boycotts. He was found guilty and sentenced to pay $500 or do 386 days of hard labor. Then came the news that the Supreme Court had declared that segregation on buses in Alabama was unconstitutional. African Americans would no longer have to sit in the back of the bus or give up their seats to anyone.

DR. KING: Here it comes.

REVEREND ABERNATHY: Right on time, too. I never thought I'd look forward to taking a bus at six o'clock in the morning.

ROSA PARKS: Over a year . . . it's hard to believe it's been that long since any of us has set foot on a Montgomery city bus.

DR. KING: Mrs. Parks, by all rights, you should be the first one of us to board that bus. We're not looking for trouble—

REVEREND ABERNATHY: But it might be looking for us.

DR. KING: I don't think there'll be any trouble. Too many eyes are turned on us today. But just in case, Mrs. Parks, it would be better if you stood between me and Reverend Abernathy as we board.

ROSA PARKS: I don't care when I board, so long as I get a seat in the front.

DR. KING: I can promise you that, Mrs. Parks. *(The bus stops. King, Parks, and Abernathy enter the bus.)* Good morning, sir.

DRIVER: *(nervously)* I don't want any trouble. Sit anywhere, anywhere at all. 'Course you can't sit *here*. This is my seat. I've got to drive the bus, after all.

DR. KING: I would like the *opportunity* to drive the bus. I would like for any African-American man or woman to have the same opportunity as you do.

DRIVER: *(mumbling)* Great, now he wants to take away my job.

DR. KING: Not if you do your job well and treat your passengers with respect. Treating us fairly won't take anything away from you at all. *(He turns to help Rosa Parks board the bus.)* Mrs. Parks, where would you like to sit today?

ROSA PARKS: I always like to sit up front by a window. *(She sits two rows behind the driver.)*

REVEREND ABERNATHY: I always like to sit on the aisle myself. *(He sits beside Rosa Parks.)*

(King sits in front of Rosa Parks. A white male passenger boards the bus and looks around.)

WHITE MALE PASSENGER: Dr. King? Is this seat taken? I'd be very proud to sit next to you.

ACT 2

SCENE 1: April 11, 1963. In King's room at the Gaston Motel in Birmingham, Alabama.

NARRATOR 1: Inspired by King's nonviolent message, college students began to stage sit-ins in the South. Lunch counters were still segregated. Black students sat at the whites-only counters and asked to be served. When they were ignored or refused service, the students opened their books and sat peacefully at the counters. They returned the next day, and the day after that. Each day more students joined them.

NARRATOR 2: The sit-ins began in 1960 in Greensboro, North Carolina, and spread throughout the South. Little by little, cities and towns began to integrate their lunch counters. In 1961, the Supreme Court declared that segregation in railroad stations and bus terminals was against the law. Restrooms and water fountains for whites only were illegal. Separate sections on trains and buses were illegal, too. The South ignored the law.

NARRATOR 3: Busloads of protesters poured into the South to protest. Birmingham, Alabama, proved to be a hard city to integrate. On April 3, 1963, Dr. King wrote the "Birmingham Manifesto." Public places should be integrated, he said, and local merchants should hire black workers. In the first week of protests in Birmingham, over 300 African Americans were put in jail.

REVEREND ABERNATHY: We're out of bail money. We can't keep up the protests if everyone's in jail. We need to have money to bail our people out. We need you to go out and raise more money, Martin. Nobody else can reach the people like you can.

DR. KING: I don't feel I can leave Birmingham now. We still don't know what Bull Connor's going to do. He's head of the police, and there's not a man in the South who's got a worse reputation than he was. Now that the Alabama court's said that the protests here are illegal, he may think that he can do anything he wants to stop us.

REVEREND ABERNATHY: What good can you do if you're in jail?

DR. KING: What if we don't continue to protest? What if we obey the state court? We'll lose too much. No, I've got to march. I've got so many people depending on me. I've got to march.

SCENE 2: April 12, 1963. At the King home in Atlanta, Georgia, and the White House in Washington, D.C.

NARRATOR 1: King, Abernathy, and 50 protesters marched to the Birmingham City Hall the next day.

NARRATOR 2: Everyone was arrested.

NARRATOR 3: For a full day, nobody knew what had happened to Martin Luther King, Jr. He was being held in a cell by himself. No one was allowed to see him. The jailers refused to let him make any phone calls. Coretta Scott King took matters into her own hands.

CORETTA: *(speaking into the telephone)* Yes, this is Coretta Scott King. I'd like to talk to President Kennedy. *(pausing to listen)* It's about my husband, Dr. Martin Luther King, Jr. He's in jail in Birmingham. No one's seen him or spoken to him in over twenty-four hours. *(pausing to listen)* Yes, I'll hold on.

ROBERT KENNEDY: Mrs. King? This is Bobby Kennedy. My brother's out of town right now. How can I help?

CORETTA: Martin's been arrested in Birmingham. I've called the jail, but they won't let me talk to him. They won't tell me how he is. They've put him in solitary confinement. No one's been able to see him or talk to him.

ROBERT KENNEDY: Bull Connor is a very hard man to deal with, Mrs. King. But I promise you that I'll look into the situation.

CORETTA: You're the Attorney General of the United States, Mr. Kennedy. Surely, Mr. Connor must listen to you.

ROBERT KENNEDY: He's ignored the Supreme Court. I imagine he'll take my call, but I can't say that he'll do what's right. I do know that President Kennedy is paying close attention to what's happening in Birmingham. We'll make sure your husband's all right.

Scene 2: April 13, 1963. Inside the Birmingham jail and the King home in Atlanta, Georgia.

GUARD 1: *(politely)* Morning, Dr. King. How's everything today? We've got a little surprise for you.

DR. KING: *(with suspicion)* What's that?

GUARD 2: You get to phone home.

DR. KING: You weren't so kind to me yesterday.

GUARD 1: We were just having some fun. A little name calling never hurt anybody.

GUARD 2: We never know what a prisoner might do. You've got to prove yourself to us. We aren't going to be buddy-buddy with a prisoner right off the bat.

DR. KING: May I have some privacy while I make my call?

GUARD 1: Anything you want, Dr. King. Anything at all.

GUARD 2: You be sure to tell them that at home, hear? Tell them how cooperative we've been down here in Birmingham.

(The guards leave the cell.)

DR. KING: *(picking up phone and dialing)* Coretta? It's Martin.

CORETTA: Martin! Are you alright? I've been so worried!

DR. KING: I'm doing pretty well.

CORETTA: President Kennedy called to tell me you were safe, but—

DR. KING: Who? Who called you?

CORETTA: The president. He said he called Birmingham. He told me you would be calling in a few minutes.

DR. KING: He called you himself? Directly?

CORETTA: Yes, and I spoke to Bobby Kennedy before that, too.

DR. KING: Get the word out, Coretta. Spread the word—the eyes of the world are on Birmingham!

ACT 3

SCENE: August 28, 1963. Washington, D.C. In the mall between the Washington Monument and the Lincoln Memorial.

NARRATOR 1: King remained in jail for eight days. During that time he wrote the "Birmingham Letter" which said that white Southerners were wrong for not obeying the Supreme Court. He also said that African Americans were right to break segregation laws. Over one million copies of the letter were distributed. The protests continued in Birmingham. Children began to take part in the marches.

NARRATOR 2: Despite King's message of nonviolence, rocks and bottles were thrown at the police one day in May. The police ordered firefighters to turn their hoses on the children. Guard dogs were sent into the crowd. Because people

saw pictures on television and in the newspapers, the whole world was horrified. A month later, President Kennedy said he was introducing a civil rights bill to Congress that promised freedom for all.

NARRATOR 3: The time was right for a parade celebrating civil rights. It was one of the biggest peaceful gatherings in the history of the U.S. The leaders of the civil rights movement joined with labor leaders and clergy to lead thousands of concerned citizens in a march on Washington for "Jobs and Freedom."

REVEREND ABERNATHY: What a turnout! This is truly inspiring!

CORETTA: Martin's speaking next. I think it's one of his finest speeches.

PHILIP RANDOLPH: And now, without any further waiting, here is the moral leader of the nation—Dr. Martin Luther King, Jr!

(The crowd cheers and applauds. King waves.)

DR. KING: Five score years ago, a great American in whose symbolic shadow we stand today, signed the Emancipation Proclamation. But 100 years later, the Negro is still not free. I have a dream.

I have a dream that one day on the red hills of Georgia, the sons of former slaves and the sons of former slave owners will be able to sit down together at the table of brotherhood . . . I have a dream that little children will one day live in a nation where they will be judged not by the color of their skins but by the content of their character. I have a dream today. I have a dream . . . one day right there in Alabama, little black boys and black girls will be able to join hands with little white boys and white girls as sisters and brothers . . . Let freedom ring!

CROWD: Let it ring! Let it ring!

DR. KING: And when this happens, when we allow freedom to ring, when we let it ring from every village and hamlet, from every state and every city, we will be able to speed up that day when all of God's children, black men and white men, Jews and Gentiles, Protestants and Catholics will be able to join hands and sing in the words of the old Negro spiritual: Free at last, free at last, thank God almighty, we're free at last . . . I have a dream . . . I have a dream.

THE END

Teacher's Guide
MARTIN LUTHER KING, JR.

QUOTES

Nonviolent resistance is not a method for cowards; it does resist. If one uses this method because he is afraid or merely because he lacks the instrument of violence, he is not truly nonviolent.

Any law that uplifts human personality is just. Any law that degrades human personality is unjust. All segregation statutes are unjust because segregation distorts the soul and damages the personality.

BIOGRAPHY

Martin Luther King, Jr. was born on January 15, 1929, in Atlanta, Georgia. He graduated from Morehouse College in 1948 and was ordained as a Baptist minister. While studying theology at Crozer Seminary in Chester, Pennsylvania, King attended a lecture on Mahatma Gandhi's nonviolent struggle for freedom for the people of India. Gandhi's teachings had a profound effect on the young Baptist minister. Upon graduation, King received a scholarship to pursue a doctoral degree at Boston University. There he met Coretta Scott, who was studying voice at the Boston Conservatory of Music. The two were married in 1953. They had four children.

King's involvement in nonviolent protest began in 1955 in Montgomery, Alabama, where he led a successful boycott of the city's buses. Over the next 13 years, he promoted nonviolence as a means for African Americans to achieve their civil rights, and was jailed several times. King also helped found the Southern Christian Leadership Conference (SCLC) in 1957. Internationally, he was viewed as an eloquent and forceful proponent of nonviolence. Among other prizes and awards given to him, King was honored with the Nobel Peace Prize in 1964. Four years later, at the age or 39, he was assassinated in Memphis, Tennessee. Today, King's birthday, January 15, is celebrated as a national holiday.

READ ABOUT HIM

* *I Have a Dream: The Life and Words of Martin Luther King, Jr.* by James Haskins (Millbrook Press, 1992)
* *Martin Luther King, Jr.* by Robert Jakoubek (Chelsea House, 1989)
* *If You Lived at the Time of Martin Luther King* by Ellen Levine (Scholastic, 1994)

TALK ABOUT HIM

A Nonviolent Solution: Conflicts arise among people almost everyday. Some are minor; others are more serious. Discuss possible sources of conflict between individuals or groups of people. Make a list of the situations that students generate. Then have pairs of students role play the conflicts and the solutions. How many different nonviolent resolutions do students create?

We Have Dreams, Too: Read aloud the entire text of the "I Have a Dream" speech that King delivered in Washington, D.C., or have students take turns reading it aloud. What are the students' dreams for America? Discuss what they think can be done to make their dreams come true.

WRITE ABOUT HIM

Another Man of Peace: The teachings of Mahatma Gandhi influenced Martin Luther King, Jr., and had a direct impact on the civil rights movement in America. Ask students to work in groups of three or four to research Gandhi's life and words and the struggle for Indian independence from England. Have them use the research to write a play about Gandhi.

In Honor of Dr. King: Many communities in the United States have named streets or buildings in honor of Martin Luther King, Jr. Have students select a public place such as a park, an airport, or a town square in which to commemorate Dr. King. They should design a statue or monument that pays tribute to the civil rights leader's achievements. Let the students present their drawings or models along with maps showing the sites they propose to the rest of the class.

Carrying on the Tradition: Although Coretta Scott was from Alabama, she met Martin Luther King, Jr., in Boston, where she was studying to become a singer. Her plans changed. She married King, and they had four children together. Coretta accompanied her husband to India, endured threats and bombings, and participated in the civil rights movement. Urge students to discover more about her life. Have them create a television documentary focusing on Coretta Scott King's life. They may incorporate photographs, quotes, and maps into their script.

THURGOOD MARSHALL
The Fight for Equal Justice
By Jacqueline Charlesworth

CHARACTERS (in order of appearance):

NARRATORS 1 AND 2

WILLIAM MARSHALL: Thurgood's father

THURGOOD MARSHALL

WILLIAM MARSHALL: Thurgood's brother

NORMA MARSHALL: Thurgood's mother

NAACP STAFF ATTORNEYS 1 AND 2

POLICE OFFICERS 1-4

JUSTICES OF THE SUPREME COURT 1-7 (nonspeaking roles)

FELIX FRANKFURTER: Justice of the Supreme Court

EARL WARREN: Chief Justice of the Supreme Court

REPORTERS 1 AND 2

LYNDON B. JOHNSON: President of the United States

INTRODUCTION

NARRATOR 1: After the Civil War, black children started going to school, but, especially in the South, they often had to attend different schools from the white children—a practice called *segregation*. The black schools often had fewer teachers and supplies than the white schools. On May 17, 1954, the Supreme Court of the United States issued an opinion that said segregation in the schools was illegal, and black children must be allowed to go to school with white children.

NARRATOR 2: Many consider this opinion, called *Brown v. Board of Education*, to be the most important decision the Supreme Court ever made. The justices on the Court had taken a stand. They said that the Constitution stood for real equality—even though they knew that many white people would be angry and would fight hard to keep black children out of "their" schools. A black man was responsible for persuading the justices to do the right thing. That man was a lawyer named Thurgood Marshall.

ACT 1

SCENE: The kitchen of a middle-class black home in Baltimore, Maryland, in 1918. Norma Marshall is at the stove. Her husband William is at the kitchen table with their son, also named William.

NARRATOR 1: Thurgood Marshall was named after his grandfather on his father's side, a former slave. His grandfather had chosen to call himself Thoroughgood when he joined the Union Army to fight against slavery during the Civil War. When the younger Thoroughgood was in second grade, he decided that his name was too long and shortened it to Thurgood.

NARRATOR 2: Thurgood's mother, Norma Arica, was a school teacher at an all-black elementary school. His father, William, worked for the Baltimore & Ohio Railroad as a dining car waiter, which was considered a good job for a black man in those days. And there was one other member of the family, Thurgood's older brother, also named William.

(Ten-year-old Thurgood trudges in and throws his schoolbooks onto the table.)

WILLIAM SR.: Why, son, what's got into you? And why are you so late in coming home?

THURGOOD: I had to stay after school again.

WILLIAM JR.: Let me guess—your big mouth got you into trouble again!

NORMA: William, right now you're the one with the big mouth. All right, Thurgood, what happened this time?

WILLIAM SR.: Norma, you know Thurgood's just a high-spirited boy. Takes after his great-grandfather, brought all the way over here from Africa. The way folks tell it, that man was so feisty, his owner had no choice but to set him free! Now, son, go on and tell us what happened.

THURGOOD: During geography, Fred leaned over and asked if I thought the kids in the white school were as bored as we were. I was just going to tell him that I didn't understand why there should be separate schools for whites, but in any case I doubted that geography could ever be interesting—when the teacher told us we'd have to stay after school because we were talking. She said that we couldn't leave until we had memorized another piece of the Constitution!

NORMA: Which piece was it this time?

THURGOOD: *(reciting from the Fourteenth Amendment)* No state shall make or enforce any law which shall abridge the privileges or immunities of citizens of the United States; nor shall any state deprive any person of life, liberty, or property, without due process of law; nor deny to any person within its jurisdiction the equal protection of the laws.

WILLIAM SR.: Do you know what that means?

THURGOOD: It seems like a long way of saying that all citizens of the United States are supposed to be treated the same under the law.

NORMA: Good for you, Thurgood! Seeing as how you take after your great-grandfather, I think you're going to know the whole Constitution before you get out of grade school. How about some supper?

ACT 2

SCENE: A dark night in Columbia, Tennessee, in 1946. Thurgood and two other NAACP lawyers are driving back to their hotel in Nashville after a long day in court.

NARRATOR 1: After graduating from college, Thurgood knew he wanted to be a lawyer. When he was turned down by the all-white University of Maryland, he enrolled in the law school of Howard University, a prestigious black institution, where he quickly became a top student.

NARRATOR 2: One of Thurgood's professors at Howard was so impressed with his student that he later offered Thurgood a job with the National Association for the Advancement of Colored People (NAACP), a group dedicated to helping black people achieve equality. As an NAACP lawyer, Thurgood traveled around the country fighting for the rights of black people in the courts. Sometimes, the job was dangerous.

THURGOOD: *(at wheel)* Whew! I would say that was a good day's work!

STAFF ATTORNEY 1: Yeah, 24 of our brothers out of jail—one to go!

STAFF ATTORNEY 2: I can't imagine what those white cops were thinking—arresting 25 men for attempted murder. It's the cops who raided a black neighborhood, not vice versa! There's not a shred of evidence against any of those defendants.

(Sound of sirens approaching)

THURGOOD: *(looking into the rear-view mirror)* Speaking of cops, we're about to get pulled over.

(As the sirens grow louder, Thurgood pulls the car over to side of road. Three police cars pull up behind, and in a moment, the lawyers' car is surrounded by four white police officers.)

OFFICER 1: Everyone out of the car! Now!

THURGOOD: Excuse me officer, but can you tell me what the problem is?

OFFICER 2: We'll let you know when we find it. Now get out!

(The three lawyers get out of the car.)

OFFICER 1: These colored lawyers think they're so smart, but I wouldn't be surprised to find out they're carrying some illegal liquor with them. Search the car, men!

(Officers 3 and 4 search car but find nothing.)

OFFICER 3: I don't see anything, boss. Just a bunch of law books and papers.

OFFICER 4: Don't you worry. We'll get 'em next time!

OFFICER 2: All right, boys, you can go on—this time—but you better hightail it out of town.

NARRATOR 1: Thurgood felt lucky that he made it back to Nashville that night. Even though the incident had shaken him up, he returned to the town of Columbia the next week to obtain the release of the last of the 25 accused black men.

SCENE 1: Inside the Supreme Court in Washington, D. C., on December 9, 1952. Nine white men in black robes sit in a row behind a high table at one end of the room. The overflow audience includes many lawyers and reporters who have come to listen to the case *Brown v. Board of Education* being argued.

THURGOOD: Your Honors, the Fourteenth Amendment of the Constitution is a guarantee of equality to negro and white children alike. There is no evidence that negro children do not have the same ability to learn as white children. What the evidence *does* show is that forcing negro children to attend separate schools hurts them because it teaches them they are not as good as white children.

JUSTICE FRANKFURTER: Mr. Marshall, don't you think we just have to recognize certain facts of life? That this is the way some people want to live?

THURGOOD: Your Honor, to accept segregation as a fact of life is to accept that negro children don't deserve full equality. The Court should make clear that that is not what our Constitution stands for.

SCENE 2: Inside the Supreme Court, about a year and a half later.

JUSTICE WARREN: *(clearing throat)* I have for announcement the judgment and opinion of the Court in *Brown v. Board of Education*, in which young negro students have challenged the constitutionality of public schools that segregate students by race.

REPORTER 1: *(whispering to Reporter 2, who's dozing off)* Hey, wake up! It's the *Brown* decision!

REPORTER 2: *(almost jumping up)* It's about time!

JUSTICE WARREN: *(continuing)* To answer the question presented by this case, we must look at the effect of segregation on public education. Today, education is perhaps the most important function of state and local governments. It is doubtful that any child may reasonably be expected to succeed in life if he is denied the opportunity of an education. Such an opportunity must be provided on equal terms. Does segregation of children in public schools solely on the basis of race deprive the children of the minority group of equal educational opportunities? *(slight pause)* We believe that it does.

REPORTER 2: *(whispering to Reporter 1 as they write quickly in their notebooks)* Wow! This is really big! The Court just struck down segregation in the schools!

WARREN: *(continuing)* To separate some children from others of similar age and qualifications solely because of their race generates a feeling of inferiority as to their status in the community that may affect their hearts and minds in a way unlikely ever to be undone. And so today we declare segregation to be unconstitutional.

ACT 4

SCENE: The White House Rose Garden, June 13, 1967. A crowd of reporters with television cameras and microphones waits for President Johnson to begin a press conference.

NARRATOR 2: After winning the *Brown* case, Thurgood continued his legal battles on behalf of African Americans. In 1961, recognizing how much Thurgood had helped shape the law in the area of civil rights, President John F. Kennedy nominated him to be a judge on a federal appeals court in New York. A few years later, President Lyndon B. Johnson chose Thurgood to be Solicitor General, a high-ranking legal position in the United States government. There was more in store for the famous civil rights lawyer.

REPORTER 2: What do you suppose this is all about? My boss told me to get here on the double.

REPORTER 1: It's got to be the Supreme Court vacancy. Wait a minute—here comes the President. Look! He's got Thurgood Marshall with him.

REPORTER 2: The Solicitor General?

PRESIDENT JOHNSON: *(standing at podium)* I have gathered you here today to announce that I am nominating Thurgood Marshall to become a Justice of the Supreme Court of the United States of America. He has served this nation well as Solicitor General, and I believe he will continue to do so on the Supreme Court.

REPORTERS 1 AND 2: *(waving hands in air)* Mr. President! Over here! Mr. President!

PRESIDENT JOHNSON: *(pointing to Reporter 1)* You there.

REPORTER 1: Mr. President, there has never before been a black man on the Supreme Court. Is that why you chose Thurgood Marshall?

PRESIDENT JOHNSON: I chose him because he deserves the appointment. Thurgood Marshall is the best qualified by training and by very valuable service to the country. (pause) I believe it is the right thing to do, the right time to do it, the right man, and the right place. (turning to Thurgood) Now, Thurgood, would you like to say a few words?

THURGOOD: *(stepping up to podium)* Mr. President, it is with great pride that I accept the honor you bestow upon me today. I will do my best to live up to it. On the front of the Supreme Court building it says "Equal Justice Under Law." I have entered that building many times and never stopped believing in those words, because in my lifetime I have seen that law can change things for the better—even the hearts of men.

THE END

Teacher's Guide
THURGOOD MARSHALL

QUOTES

I don't know of any president who ever came out, four-square, for ending all segregation in all places. I think it would be good for a president to say, 'People are all people. Take the skin off, there's no difference.' I think it would be good to say so.

I think the Constitution is the greatest body of laws ever, and what to me and to many people is so extraordinary about it is that in this late day you find that it works. I don't know of any better job that could have been done . . . . If you read it with any understanding, there's hardly anything that it doesn't cover.

BIOGRAPHY

Thurgood Marshall was born Thoroughgood Marshall on July 2, 1908, in West Baltimore, Maryland. After graduating with honors from Lincoln University, the nation's oldest black college, Thurgood went to law school at Howard University. While at Howard, he married Vivian Burey, otherwise known as "Buster."

In 1936, Charles Houston asked Thurgood to join him as an NAACP staff attorney; Thurgood took over as head lawyer in 1938. During his years as a civil rights advocate, Thurgood won the majority of the cases he argued before the Supreme Court, including *Brown v. Board of Education*, the landmark 1954 decision outlawing racial segregation in public schools. Soon after the *Brown* victory, Thurgood's wife died of cancer. He married his second wife, Cecilia Suyat, an NAACP secretary, at the end of 1955.

In 1961, President John F. Kennedy appointed Thurgood to be a judge on the United States Court of Appeals of the Second Circuit. Thurgood served on that court until 1965, when President Lyndon B. Johnson chose him to be Solicitor General. In 1967, President Johnson nominated Thurgood to be a justice of the United States Supreme Court. He retired in 1991, but left his mark as an ardent defender of the rights of minorities and women. When asked by a reporter why he was stepping down, Marshall said he was "getting old and coming apart." Thurgood Marshall died of heart failure in Bethesda, Maryland, on January 24, 1993.

READ ABOUT HIM

♦ *Brown v. Board of Education* by Harvey Fireside and Sarah Betsey Fuller (Enslow Publications, 1994)

♦ *Thurgood Marshall: A Life for Justice* by James Haskins (Henry Holt and Company, 1992)

♦ *Thurgood Marshall: Champion for Justice* by G.S. Prentzes (Chelsea House, 1993)

TALK ABOUT HIM

Equality for All: Review the examples of racism in the play—for example, segregated schools or the behavior of the white police. Talk about instances of racism or discrimination that your students have experienced or witnessed. What kinds of remedies can they think of to apply to those situations?

A Positive Punishment: When Thurgood Marshall misbehaved in grade school, the principal would make him memorize a part of the Constitution. Emphasizing the positive impact that had on Thurgood's life, have kids memorize (or read) a line or two of the Constitution. After they recite the lines to the class, they can then explain the meaning in their own words.

WRITE ABOUT HIM

A Brief Appearance: Before lawyers argue cases before the Supreme Court, they give the justices written versions of their arguments, called *briefs*, so the justices are familiar with the points of their arguments. Ask students to help Thurgood Marshall prepare his brief against segregation. They should include at least three arguments against segregation. (Hint: Because the best briefs are logical and well-organized, students might want to use a five-paragraph format: an introduction, one paragraph discussing each reason, and a summary.)

A Long Time in Coming: Thurgood Marshall helped change the role of African Americans in our society. Have students create timelines depicting landmarks in the struggle for black equality. They may wish to start with the Emancipation Proclamation in 1863 and continue to the Million Man March in Washington, D.C. After students compare and discuss their timelines, ask them to compile their information into one class timeline.

ROSA PARKS
The Fight for Equal Rights
By Beth Sherman

CHARACTERS (in order of appearance):

NARRATOR

ROSA PARKS

BLACK MALE PASSENGER

BLACK FEMALE PASSENGERS 1 AND 2

WHITE FEMALE PASSENGER

JAMES BLAKE: White bus driver

POLICE OFFICERS 1–3

RAYMOND "PARKS" PARKS: Rosa's husband

E.D. NIXON: President of the Mobile chapter of the NAACP (National Association for the Advancement of Colored People)

FRED GRAY: Black lawyer in Mobile, Alabama

JO ANN ROBINSON: Head of the Women's Political Council

MEMBERS OF THE WOMEN'S POLITICAL COUNCIL 1–3

DR. MARTIN LUTHER KING, JR.: Baptist preacher and leader of Montgomery bus boycott

REVEREND RALPH ABERNATHY: Baptist preacher and activist

CHURCH CROWD 1-5

ACT 1

SCENE 1: December 1, 1955. Inside a city bus in Montgomery, Alabama.

NARRATOR: Before 1955, racial segregation was legal in many southern states. When they rode the bus, African Americans were required to sit in the back, in the "colored section," even if there were empty seats up front. If all the "white seats" were filled, blacks were supposed to give up their seats and stand in the back. One winter night, a woman named Rosa Parks changed that forever.

(Rosa gets on the bus and sits in the middle section, next to a black man. Two other black women are seated across the aisle.)

ROSA: Good evening.

BLACK MALE PASSENGER: Evening, Mrs. Parks. Rough day today?

ROSA: Yes. It feels good to sit down. I've been bent over the steam press at the department store for hours. My shoulders and neck ache so!

BLACK FEMALE PASSENGER 1: Excuse me, Mrs. Parks. Do you know when the NAACP will be electing new officers?

WHITE FEMALE PASSENGER *(as she leaves the bus)*: NAACP, NAACP! I am sick and tired of hearing about that N-double A-CP all the time. National Association for the Advancement of Colored People—what in the world does that mean?

BLACK FEMALE PASSENGER 2: It means just what it says. It means not having to sit in the back of the bus.

ROSA: I just put the notices in the mail. We'll be holding elections next week.

(The bus stops. Several white people get on. The three black passengers get up and move to the back of the bus. Rosa doesn't move. All the whites sit down, except one man, who cannot find a seat.)

JAMES BLAKE: *(to Rosa)* Hey, you. Are you going to get up and give the gentleman your seat?

ROSA: *(softly)* No.

JAMES BLAKE: If you don't get up this minute, I'm calling the cops, and I'll have you dragged off to jail!

ROSA: *(calmly)* I'm not moving. I paid my fare, and I'm entitled to sit right here.

JAMES BLAKE: We'll see about that. *(He whistles to two policemen who are walking down the street. The policemen board the bus.)* Officer, that colored lady won't give up her seat.

OFFICER 1: *(to Rosa)* You don't look white to me. *(pulling Rosa to her feet)* Stand up.

ROSA: Why do you all push us around?

OFFICER 2: Because it's the law.

ROSA: Then the law's wrong.

OFFICER 1: Oh, so now you're a lawyer.

OFFICER 2: I don't know—could be she's a judge. Come on, judge, you're still under arrest.

(The officers escort Rosa off the bus.)

SCENE 2: Later that evening. Inside the Montgomery city jail.

NARRATOR: Rosa was taken to jail where she was fingerprinted and her mug shot was taken. Then she was placed in a dark, empty jail cell.

ROSA: I'd like to make a telephone call.

OFFICER 1: I'd like to make a million dollars.

ROSA: I'd like to call my husband to let him know I'm here.

OFFICER 2: Sorry, lady you should've thought of that *before* you broke the law.

ROSA: There's something wrong when the law doesn't treat *all* people as equal.

OFFICER 1: Yeah? Tell it to the judge.

OFFICER 3: Hey, you know who she is? She works for that E.D. Nixon guy over at the NAACP. He's been helping colored people to register to vote.

OFFICER 1: *(laughing)* What for?

OFFICER 3: Let her use the phone. What harm can it do? Here. *(handing Rosa the telephone receiver through the bars)*

ROSA: *(dialing)* Thank you. Hello, Parks. It's me. I'm in jail. *(pause)* No, I'm all right. I'll explain later. *(pause)* No, they didn't hurt me. Just come and get me out as soon as you can.

ACT 2

SCENE 1: Later that night. In the Parks' living room.

NARRATOR: Raymond Parks, Rosa's husband, along with E.D. Nixon of the NAACP, and Clifford Durr, a white lawyer who fought against segregation laws, went to jail to pick her up. As word of Rosa's arrest spread, the entire black community was angered over what had happened to her.

ROSA: I recognized that bus driver. He's the same one who put me off a bus 12 years ago, because I got on at the front, instead of using the rear door.

RAYMOND PARKS: Are you sure it's the same man?

ROSA: Yes. I'll never forget his face. He's tall, and there's a mole near his mouth.

RAYMOND PARKS: This time, things will be different.

ROSA: I'll tell you one thing—I'm never going to ride another segregated bus— even if I have to walk to work!

E.D. NIXON: Rosa, I need to ask you something. I've known you for a long time. A lot of people in these parts know you, too. They know you're an honest, hard-working woman. You have integrity. You stand up for what you believe in. That makes what happened to you a perfect test case against bus segregation. Will you help all of us?

ROSA: You bet I will!

FRED GRAY: I called Jo Ann Robinson and told her you were arrested. She got in touch with other leaders of the Women's Political Council, and they're calling for a boycott of the buses. It's due to start Monday, the same day as your trial.

E.D. NIXON: I'm going to call the local ministers, too. They'll help us get the word out.

FRED GRAY: Make sure you call the Reverend Martin Luther King, Jr. He's pastor of the Dexter Avenue Baptist Church.

ROSA: I've heard he's a powerful speaker.

NIXON: That he is. With you and the Reverend King in our corner, we're going to give them one heck of a fight.

SCENE 2: December 2, 1955. A street corner in Montgomery.

NARRATOR: The next day, members of the Women's Political Council passed out 35,000 handbills describing the boycott.

JO ANN ROBINSON: Have you heard the news? A negro woman has been arrested and put in jail because she refused to give up her seat!

WOMAN 1: Don't ride the bus on Monday! Hit the bus company where it hurts the most—their pockets!

WOMAN 2: If you have to get to work, take a cab, share a ride or walk!

WOMAN 3: Come to our meeting Monday night at the Holt Street Baptist Church. Find out how to fight back!

ACT 3

SCENE: December 5, 1955. Inside the Holt Street Baptist Church.

NARRATOR: That Monday morning, Rosa went to court, where she was convicted of breaking the segregation law and fined $14. But the boycott had begun, and it was a success. The buses were practically empty! Black people walked long distances to work, forming carpools, sharing taxis, riding bicycles. Some

even rode horses and mules. That night, people who wanted to hear more about the boycott went to the Holt Street Baptist Church. The main speaker was a 26-year-old preacher named Martin Luther King, Jr.

DR. KING: There comes a time when people get tired. We are here this evening to say to those who have mistreated us so long that we are tired—tired of being segregated and humiliated; tired of being kicked about by the brutal feet of oppression.

(The crowd cheers.)

DR. KING: We must stick together and keep the boycott going. We will fight for our rights—not with violence, but with patience. And we will triumph. If we are wrong, the Supreme Court of this nation is wrong. If we are wrong, God Almighty is wrong. If we are wrong, justice is a lie!

(The crowd cheers.)

DR. KING: And now the Reverend Ralph Abernathy will read the list of demands that the Montgomery Improvement Association is going to give the bus company and the city's white leaders.

REVEREND ABERNATHY: Thank you, Dr. King. There are three demands. Number one is courteous treatment on buses. Demand two is first come, first served seating. And number three is hiring of black drivers for black bus routes. Please stand up if you agree with these demands.

(The crowd stands up and shouts Amen.)

REVEREND ABERNATHY: And now, let's show our gratitude to Mrs. Rosa Parks.

(The crowd cheers.)

NARRATOR: The Montgomery bus boycott continued for more than a year. White terrorists tried to frighten the boycotters. They threw bottles at people walking to work. Some homes were bombed. But at last, the U.S. Supreme Court ruled that Alabama's bus segregation laws were unconstitutional. Justice was set in motion by one brave woman—Rosa Parks—who refused to give up her seat, who fought for what she believed in.

THE END

Teacher's Guide
ROSA PARKS

QUOTES

The only tired I was, was tired of giving in.

I was a regular person, just as good as anybody else.

Everyone living together in peace and harmony and love . . . that's the goal we seek.

BIOGRAPHY

Rosa Parks was born on February 4, 1913, in Tuskegee, Alabama. Her father was a carpenter; her mother was a teacher. In 1932, Rosa married Raymond Parks. Like her husband, she was a member of the National Association for the Advancement of Colored People (NAACP) and fought for the right to become a registered voter.

One night in December 1955, Rosa Parks was riding a bus home from work when she refused to give up her seat to a white man. She was arrested and jailed for two-and-a-half hours, then convicted of breaking the segregation law and fined $14. She lost her job as a seamstress in a department store. The people of Montgomery rallied behind her by boycotting the bus company. Led by Martin Luther King, Jr., the protest continued for more than a year, until the U.S. Supreme Court declared that Alabama's bus segregation laws were unconstitutional.

After the boycott, Rosa and her family moved to Detroit, Michigan, where her husband died in 1977. In 1987, she started the Raymond and Rosa Parks Institute for Self-Development, an organization to teach young people how to help themselves and their communities. Rosa Parks was also elected to the board of the NAACP. Because of her courage and determination, Rosa Parks is known as the "Mother of the Civil Rights Movement."

READ ABOUT HER

- *Rosa Parks* by Eloise Greenfield, illustrated by Eric Marlow (Thomas Y. Crowell, 1973)
- *Rosa Parks: My Story* by Rosa Parks with James Haskins (Dial Books, 1992)
- *The Year They Walked: Rosa Parks and the Montgomery Bus Boycott* by Beatrice Siegal (Macmillan, 1992)

TALK ABOUT HER

Making a Difference: Rosa Parks's refusal to give up her seat on a city bus set off a chain reaction of events—from a bus boycott to a landmark decision by the Supreme Court. One woman's actions reverberated throughout her community and eventually the entire country. Discuss with students whether or not they feel that one person can make a difference in fighting injustice. Ask them to share their opinions about other role models whom they think have made a difference in their community, the country, or the world.

Discrimination Day: Rosa Parks and the African-American citizens of Montgomery experienced discrimination first hand. Have your students ever been discriminated against because of who they are? If so, was it age, race, gender, or something else that sparked the discrimination? What did they do, or what would they liked to have done, to protest the discrimination? Would a boycott against the offending party have been practical? You may also want to hold a Discrimination Day in your class. Based on some arbitrary criteria, deny some students basic rights. For instance, everyone in your class who's wearing a blue shirt may have to sit at a separate table in the cafeteria or use a water fountain in a different part of the building.

WRITE ABOUT HER

Dear Rosa Parks: Rosa Parks is considered to be the "Mother of the Civil Rights Movement." Let students compose letters to Mrs. Parks. They may wish to applaud her courage, ask her questions about her life, or find out more about the Rosa and Raymond Parks Institute for Self-Development.

Civil Rights Hall of Fame: Rosa Parks, Dr. Martin Luther King, Jr., and Ralph Abernathy were active in the civil rights movement. Students can set up their own Civil Rights Hall of Fame in the classroom. Set aside space in the classroom for the Hall of Fame. Books such as *Freedom's Children* by Ellen Levine and *The Civil Rights Movement: The History of Black People in America, 1930-1980* by Stuart A. Kallen and Rosemary Wallner can provide information on more activists. A student can nominate someone for the Hall of Fame by preparing a report highlighting the person's role in the civil rights movement.

JACKIE ROBINSON
In a League of His Own
By Eric James Charlesworth

CHARACTERS (in order of appearance):

NARRATORS 1 AND 2

JACKIE ROBINSON: Baseball player

JIMMY: Jackie's teammate on the Kansas City Monarchs

BRANCH RICKEY: President of the Brooklyn Dodgers

PEE WEE REESE: Jackie's teammate on the Brooklyn Dodgers

PHILLIES FANS 1-3

WILLIAM BLACK: President of the Chock Full O'Nuts restaurant chain

ACT 1

SCENE: 1945. Inside the cramped bus of the Kansas City Monarchs traveling through the Midwest.

NARRATOR 1: The Kansas City Monarchs was a baseball team in the Negro League. This league, founded in 1920, was composed of black players only. Even after fighting in World War II, African Americans were forbidden to play major-league baseball. A city councilman in New York who thought this law ridiculous said: "Good enough to die for his country, but not good enough for organized baseball."

NARRATOR 2: Jackie Robinson was a young shortstop on the Monarchs. He was a terrific ballplayer, but was unhappy about the treatment of black baseball teams. Unlike major league players, he and the other players in the Negro League had to put up with long bus rides, poor playing fields, and racial prejudice. They were often refused rooms in hotels and denied service in restaurants.

JACKIE: We've been on this stupid bus forever. Hey, Jimmy, do you have any bread or anything?

JIMMY: Are you kidding? I don't have enough scraps to feed a tomcat.

JACKIE: I'm starving. I'm so sick of this whole scene—I don't know how much longer I can put up with it.

JIMMY: You're black. You want to play baseball. What other choice do you have?

JACKIE: We deserve better than this. I'm tired of getting treated like dirt. Half of us could be playing in the majors. Everybody knows that. And I don't mean just playing—I mean playing well!

JIMMY: I know how you feel, but, like I said—what choice do we have?

JACKIE: I really don't know. But I'm telling you, Jimmy, the only reason I'm sticking this out is pure and simple: I love to play the game.

JIMMY: They'll never take our mits from us, right Jack? How about we have a catch the next time we stop?

JACKIE: You'd better keep an eye on your mit, just in case.

ACT 2

SCENE: 1947 in New York City. Inside the office of Branch Rickey, president of the Brooklyn Dodgers.

NARRATOR 1: Branch Rickey, head of the Brooklyn Dodgers, asked Jackie Robinson to come to his office for what would become a very famous meeting.

NARRATOR 2: As a college baseball coach, Rickey had seen first hand the damages of racial discrimination. A hotel manager wouldn't let one of his players, Charlie Thomas, have a room. The reason? Charlie Thomas was an African American. Rickey managed to get a cot set up in his own room for Thomas. He never forgot the humiliation that the young baseball player had to face.

BRANCH: Do you know why I asked to see you here today, Jackie?

JACKIE: I know you've had scouts out looking at players in our league. The word is you're forming a team of black players.

BRANCH: No, you're not a candidate for the Brown Dodgers *or* the Brown Bombers. I want you to play for my Brooklyn Dodgers.

JACKIE: *(laughing in disbelief)* Do you really think that a black man would be accepted in the majors, Mr. Rickey?

BRANCH: Not any black man. He's got to be a solid player—better than a solid player. And no, I don't think that even the greatest player the world has ever seen would be accepted right away. I do know that you're a good enough ballplayer. What I don't know is whether or not you have the guts. Fans are going to boo you and call you names. Players are going to spike you and throw the ball at your head. This won't work if you're not able to control your temper.

JACKIE: Mr. Rickey, do you want a ballplayer who's afraid to fight back?

BRANCH: I want a guy with guts enough *not* to fight back. Do you understand?

JACKIE: Yes I do. If I get punched in the cheek, I turn the other cheek.

BRANCH: That's exactly right. Everything depends on you, Jackie. You can't slip up, not even once.

ACT 3

SCENE: 1947. Ebbetts Field in Brooklyn, home of the Dodgers. The Dodgers are playing the Philadelphia Phillies.

NARRATOR 1: Jackie Robinson's first year in the majors was a tense one. Opposing players and fans did their best to make Jackie's entry into baseball as difficult as possible. When the Phillies came to town to play the Brooklyn Dodgers, that team was no exception. Phillies' manager Ben Chapman encouraged his players to harass Jackie Robinson during the game.

PEE WEE: What's up, Jackie? You don't look so good.

JACKIE: That's 'cause I'm not so good. I've gotten death threats. They even threaten my family. I'm trying to keep my head on straight, but it's not easy.

PEE WEE: I can't even imagine what you must be going through. A whole lot of people's hopes and dreams are riding on your shoulders, and the rest of them want you out of the way. Listen—I just want you to know that no matter what happens, I'll be standing here next to you—as a teammate and a friend.

NARRATOR 2: Jackie appreciated Pee Wee's support, but dealing with the Phillies and their fans was one of the greatest challenges he would face. In Jackie's first at-bat, he hit a double. While he stood on second base, abuse was heaped on him from every direction.

PHILLIES FAN 1: Hey, boy! Go home, and clean toilets like you were meant to!

PHILLIES FAN 2: Yeah! Go back to the cotton fields! You got no business bein' on this field!

PHILLIES FAN 3: Hey Jerky—oops! I mean Jackie—you're a bum!

NARRATOR 1: Jackie remained silent at second base as Pee Wee Reese went up to bat.

PEE WEE: Listen, you yellow-bellied cowards! Jackie's kickin' your butts up and down this field. He won't answer back because he's got ten times the class any of you idiots will ever have!

NARRATOR 2: Pee Wee Reese then hit a single and Jackie scored the game-

winning run. More importantly, by keeping his gutsy calm, Jackie had scored respect for himself and for baseball. Ben Chapman's plan had backfired. The incident was reported in newspapers across the country, and support for Jackie was strong.

ACT 4

SCENE: 1957. Inside the New York City office of William Black, president of Chock Full O'Nuts, a restaurant chain.

NARRATOR 1: In 1955, Jackie Robinson accomplished his final goal of winning the World Series. That year the Dodgers beat the Yankees. The next year, the Dodgers announced that Ebbets Field had been sold, and they were moving to California.

NARRATOR 2: There was even more news: Jackie had been traded to the San Francisco Giants. The Giants offered Robinson a salary of $60,000, a tremendous amount of money at the time, but Jackie refused. It was time to retire from baseball. He was ready to move into the world of business.

JACKIE: V.P. of Community Relations sounds good, but what does that mean? Am I just a name to you? Or are you going to let me really *do* something?

WILLIAM: No sir, I expect a great deal from you. You've said that you don't want to have a title that doesn't mean anything. And I don't want to have a man with a title who's not doing anything for my company but signing baseballs.

JACKIE: *(nodding)* I think we understand each other.

NARRATOR 1: Jackie was finished proving himself as an athlete and as a man. Thanks to his courage and strength, the major leagues were integrated. As the boos turned to cheers, Jackie opened the door for many black players, from Willie Mays to Ken Griffey Jr. Besides being successful in business, he continued to fight for equality by becoming involved in politics, and serving as a spokesperson for the NAACP.

NARRATOR 2: Baseball is often called America's favorite past-time. But baseball was never truly American until Jackie Robinson joined the Brooklyn Dodgers.

THE END

Teacher's Guide
JACKIE ROBSINSON

QUOTES

I guess if I could choose one of the most important moments in my life, I would go back to 1947, in the Yankee Stadium in New York City. It was the opening day of the World Series and I was for the first time playing in the series as a member of the Brooklyn Dodgers team.

I want to be free to follow the dictates of my own mind and conscience without being subject to the pressures of any man, black or white. I think that is what most people of all races want.

A life is not important, except in the impact it has on other lives.

BIOGRAPHY

Jack Roosevelt Robinson was born on January 31, 1919 to parents who share-cropped on a Georgia plantation. When Jackie was young, his father left home, and soon after, his mother moved the family to California. Jackie attended Pasadena Junior College before moving on to UCLA. There, he was a star in baseball, football, track, and basketball. Some people labeled him "the finest athlete in America." While in school, Jackie met Rachel Isum, whom he later married. He left UCLA before graduating to support his mother, then entered the army, where he as a Lieutenant during World War II. After being discharged, Robinson joined the Kansas City Monarchs and played in the Negro Baseball League. In 1947, he was asked to play for the Brooklyn Dodgers, thus becoming the first black to play major league baseball. During his career with the Dodgers, Jackie won Rookie of the Year and Most Valuable Player Awards and led the team to a World Series title in 1955.

He retired in 1957, In 1962, in his first year of eligibility, he was the first African American inducted into the Baseball Hall of Fame. After retiring from baseball, he was instrumental in working for political change as a member of the NAACP. Jackie Robinson died in 1972 at the age of 53.

READ ABOUT HIM

♦ *Black Diamond: The Story of the Negro Baseball Leagues* by Patricia and Frederick C. McKissack, Jr. (Scholastic, 1994)

♦ *Jackie Robinson* by Richard Scott (Chelsea House Publishers, 1987)

♦ *Jackie Robinson* by Manfred Weidhorn (Atheneum, 1994)

TALK ABOUT HIM

Decisions, Decisions: In making major decisions, we usually compose a list of pros and cons. What do students think might have been on Jackie Robinson's list when he was offered the position on the Brooklyn Dodgers? What might have been on Branch Rickey's list when he thought about hiring African-American players for the Dodgers?

Standing Up for a Friend: Pee Wee Reese was not only a teammate of Jackie Robinson's, he was also a friend. Reese stood beside Robinson in some difficult times. Ask students to define the qualities that make someone a good friend. Have they ever been in situations where friends stood up for them, or they stood up for their friends?

WRITE ABOUT HIM

In My Opinion: After the Dodgers played the Phillies, many national newspapers were filled with stories of the Phillies' bad behavior. Editorials lambasted the Phillies, their manager, and their fans. Ask students to write a news story or an editorial about the incident.

The Negro Baseball League: Before Jackie Robinson broke the color barrier in baseball, African-American players had formed their own league, the Negro Baseball League. Have students find out more about the players and the league. They may wish to focus on individual players, teams, or the history of the league itself. Ask students to present their research in the form of an article for a sports magazine.

Trading Cards: From his days with the Kansas City Monarchs to his retirement from the Brooklyn Dodgers, Jackie Robinson's career was highlighted by honors. Encourage groups of students to design baseball cards for different years in Robinson's career. They should include a photo or illustration of Robinson on the front of the card and biographical and statistical information on the back.

SOJOURNER TRUTH
Living Up to Her Name

By Lynda D. Jones

CHARACTERS (in order of appearance):

NARRATORS 1 AND 2

MA-MA BETT: Sojourner's mother

SOJOURNER TRUTH: Known as Isabelle, or Belle, in her early years

PETER: Sojourner's brother

MRS. SCHRYVER: Tavern owner

JOHN DUMONT: Sojourner's owner

ISAAC VAN WAGENER: Quaker man

PETER: Sojourner's son

JUDGE

QUAKER WOMAN

WOMAN AT CONVENTION

MRS. FRANCES GAGE: Women's rights leader

ABRAHAM LINCOLN: 16th President of the United States

ACT 1

SCENE 1: 1806. Midnight, in the cellar of a mansion in Ulster County, New York.

NARRATOR 1: Sojourner Truth was born into slavery in the year 1797. Her real name was Isabella, but her parents James and Ma-Ma called her Belle. James and Ma-Ma had ten children. All of the children had been sold into slavery by the time Belle was born. Now only Belle and her younger brother Peter lived with their parents.

NARRATOR 2: The family lived with 12 other slaves in a cold and damp cellar under a mansion. Belle spoke Dutch and knew no English. Like many enslaved people, Belle wasn't taught how to read or write. But she loved listening to the stories Ma-Ma told—even though they were often sad.

MA-MA: It was snowing outside. A white man drove up in a red sleigh and went inside the master's house. Michael and Nancy heard the sleigh bells and ran outside. *(She pauses.)*

PETER: Go on. Then what happened, Ma-Ma?

MA-MA: Your brother Michael was only five then. He climbed into the sleigh because he thought the man would take him for a ride. When the man came out of the house, he hauled your sister Nancy into the sleigh. Michael was dancing up and down, up and down, because *he* wanted to ride in the sleigh.

PETER: *I* would have jumped right up on that sleigh and gotten a ride!

BELLE: No, you wouldn't. Not if you ever wanted to see us again.

PETER: What does she mean, Ma-Ma?

MA-MA: The man shoved my Nancy inside a box in back of the sleigh. He slammed the lid down and bolted it shut. Michael tried to run away then, but the man caught him and put him in the box, too. I could hear my babies crying and calling for me. I tried to run after the man, but they wouldn't let me. Your father did all he could . . . but our babies were gone.

BELLE: That's never going to happen to me or Peter. I promise, Ma-Ma.

MA-MA: I don't know where eight of my children are. We look at the same stars at night, but I don't know where they are. *(She takes a deep breath to calm herself.)* There is something you can promise me, Belle. You, too, Peter. Don't let white folks ever see what *you* feel or think. Work hard. Be loyal. Promise me?!

SCENE 2: 1809. A tavern on the Rondout River in New York.

NARRATOR 1: In 1808, Belle was sold, at the age of 11, along with a flock of sheep for $100. She was bought by John Neely, an English storekeeper. Angry that Belle spoke only Dutch, her new owners treated her badly.

NARRATOR 2: One day, James managed to visit his daughter. He had sad news for Belle: Ma-Ma had passed away. Seeing that Belle had to go barefoot in the snow, and how she'd been beaten, her father promised to help her. He convinced Martin Schryver, a fisherman and tavern owner, to buy Belle from the Neelys. The Schryvers spoke both Dutch and English, so Belle was finally able to learn English. Working in the tavern, she heard the word *abolition* for the first time.

BELLE: Mr. Schryver said that that man over there was an abolitionist. What does that mean? Is it the kind of work he does?

MRS. SCHRYVER: *(surprised)* You've never heard that word before? An abolitionist is someone who wants to end slavery.

BELLE: Then I'm an abolitionist.

MRS. SCHRYVER: You'd better be careful who you say that to, else you'll get yourself into a lot of trouble. You'll be free when you're twenty-five years old. That's what the state of New York says. *(She goes to wait on a customer.)*

BELLE: That's too long to wait.

ACT 2

SCENE 1: 1826. The Van Wageners' home.

NARRATOR 1: The Schryvers sold Belle to John Dumont. Tall and strong, she did the work of a man and a woman. In the morning, she would go out into the fields to take care of the land. In the afternoon, she would wash clothes, cook, and clean. When Dumont thought it was time for Belle to have a family, he

married her to Thomas, an enslaved man on his farm. They had five children. Dumont promised Belle that if she continued to work hard, he would free her and Thomas one year before Freedom Day.

NARRATOR 2: Freedom Day was July 4, 1827. On that day, all enslaved people born before 1799 were to go free. Dumont either didn't or couldn't keep his promise. He told Belle that she was too valuable to him to let her go, so she took her youngest daughter, Sophia, and ran away. The Van Wageners, a Quaker family, took Belle in. Dumont tracked her down.

DUMONT: Well, Belle, so you've run away from me.

BELLE: I didn't run...I *walked* away by daylight, and all because you had promised to free me one year ahead of schedule. You weren't true to your word.

DUMONT: You must come back with me, Belle.

BELLE: No, I won't go back with you.

DUMONT: Well, I shall take the child.

VAN WAGENER: No! If money is all you understand, then I'll give you $25: twenty for Belle and five for Sophia. *(He looks at Belle.)* If that's all right with you.

BELLE: I'll stay. I'm a hard worker. You won't be sorry you helped us.

DUMONT: *(confused and surprised)* But you're a Quaker. You don't believe in buying and selling people.

VAN WAGENER: I don't believe in keeping some people from being free. If I have to pay to make someone free, then I will.

SCENE 2: Judge's chambers in the Kingston, New York, courthouse.

NARRATOR 1: Belle and her daughter Sophia were safe, but Mr. Dumont sold her son Peter. She learned that Peter would be sent to England. Those plans changed, but her son was still taken far away from her to Alabama.

NARRATOR 2: The law in New York State at that time outlawed any out-of-state selling of slaves. Aided by the Van Wageners and other Quakers, Belle

sued for the return of Peter. The jury decided in Belle's favor. This was a first: an African-American woman going through the legal system and winning. There was a catch, however: Peter didn't want to return to his mother.

PETER: She's not my mother! I'm not going with her!

BELLE: You remember me—I know you do. Don't you remember how we—

PETER: NO!

JUDGE: Calm down, son. Tell me: How did you get that scar on your forehead?

PETER: (*looking scared*) A horse kicked me.

JUDGE: (*to Belle*) Did he have that scar when you last saw him?

BELLE: No, your honor, nor the one on his cheek there.

JUDGE: (*to Peter*) How did you get that scar on your cheek?

PETER: (*looking more scared*) I . . . it was a carriage. I ran into a carriage door.

BELLE: (*going toward her son*) My poor, poor boy. What have they done to you?

PETER: No! No! I won't leave my master! I won't! He's good to me! He is!

JUDGE: Son, you're safe in here. There's no need for you to lie. No one's going to hurt you anymore. You're going home with your mother.

PETER: (*relaxing a little*) Maybe . . . maybe she does look a bit like my mother.

ACT 3

SCENE 1: June 1, 1843. Morning, in front of a Quaker farm east of New York City.

NARRATOR 1: Hoping to get a job for herself and a good education for her son, Belle and Peter moved to New York City. Unfortunately, Peter got into trouble and was jailed. After his release, he went to sea. Peter wrote to his mother to apologize for all the trouble he had caused. His letters eventually stopped, and Belle never heard from him again.

NARRATOR 2: Life in the city was hard. People competed for jobs, education, and housing. One day, Belle woke up and decided to go west. She changed her name, too—a name that had never really been hers. Sojourner Truth was born.

SOJOURNER: *(stopping at gate)* Please, missus, could you spare some water?

QUAKER WOMAN: The well is over by the corner of the house. Help yourself.

SOJOURNER: Thank you, missus.

QUAKER WOMAN: What's your name, dear?

SOJOURNER: Sojourner Truth. The Bible says a sojourner is a person who moves from place to place. I'm heading west to find the truth.

SCENE 2: 1851. Akron, Ohio, where a women's rights convention is being held in a church.

NARRATOR 1: True to her name, Sojourner traveled through the North singing hymns, preaching about the evils of slavery, and caring for the sick. She made friends of writers, former slaves, and abolitionists, such as Frederick Douglass. Soon Sojourner became well known, and people gathered to hear her speak about her life as a slave. Her words touched everyone who listened.

NARRATOR 2: One day, Sojourner met a woman who suggested that she publish the story of her life. Sojourner agreed. *The Narrative of Sojourner Truth: A Northern Slave* was published in 1850. She hoped that her experiences would inspire the slaves in the South. Sojourner became such a prominent speaker that her peers encouraged her to speak out at another convention.

WOMAN: *(whispering to Mrs. Gage)* Don't let her speak! The newspapers will mix women's rights causes with Negroes and antislavery. We'll lose support!

MRS. GAGE: We'll see what we lose. Friends, please welcome Sojourner Truth!

(Many in the crowd hiss and jeer as Sojourner starts to speak.)

SOJOURNER: Well children, there's so much racket around here something must be out of kilter. Between the Negroes and the women in the North, white men will be in a fix. *(pointing her finger at a man in the crowd)* That man over there says that women need to be helped over ditches and into carriages. Not

me. And aren't I a woman? I've plowed, planted and worked in the barn. No man could do better than me. I could work as hard and eat as much as a man, and bear whippings from my slave master. And aren't I a woman? I have borne children and seen them sold into slavery, and cried out with a mother's grief.

 ACT 4

SCENE: October 29, 1864. The White House.

NARRATOR 1: Sojourner continued to travel throughout Kansas, Indiana, and Ohio preaching about equality for African Americans and women. In 1863, hoping to bring an end to the Civil War, President Abraham Lincoln signed the Emancipation Proclamation which freed all enslaved people in the United States.

NARRATOR 2: Sojourner traveled to Washington, D.C., to speak to President Lincoln. She wanted to urge him to do more for the newly freed people; but when she saw his exhausted face, she changed her mind.

LINCOLN: I would say welcome to my home, but it is yours as much as mine.

SOJOURNER: I don't have much use for a home these days, Mr. President. I have to live up to my name.

LINCOLN: (nodding) It's a fine name, too. We know it well in the Midwest. Many people have passed through my door here, but you are one of the few I have had a longing to meet.

SOJOURNER: Can't say I've heard of you before you moved to the White House.

LINCOLN: (laughing) There's more that wish they'd never heard the sound of my name! (looking at the scrapbook Sojourner holds in her lap) What's this?

SOJOURNER: My "Book of Life." Newspaper clippings, drawings, pictures, letters, autographs of some of the folks I've met in my time. Would you mind signing?

LINCOLN: Not at all. Just tell me the truth: How am I doing as your president.

SOJOURNER: Like Daniel in the lion's den, Mr. President. You'll win in the end.

 THE END

Teacher's Guide
SOJURNER TRUTH

QUOTES

It seems I am going to battle. But I carry no weapon. The lord will preserve me without weapons. I feel safe even in the midst of my enemies, for the truth is all-powerful and will prevail.

I am not ready to be writ up yet, for I have still lots to accomplish.

BIOGRAPHY

Sojourner Truth was born into slavery in 1797 in Hurley, Ulster County New York. Her given name was Isabella, and she was called Belle. Each of her nine brothers and sisters were taken away and sold. At the age of 11, Belle herself was separated from her family and sold at auction. Sold several more times after that, she was often treated cruelly and beaten. In 1826, Belle took her freedom. With her youngest son, Peter, she moved to New York City, where she found several of her lost brothers and sisters. In 1846, Belle changed her name to Sojourner Truth and left the city. She began to speak at church meetings about her experiences, and soon became an important member of the abolitionist movement.

In 1850 a friend helped her publish a book about her life. The book was called *Narrative of Sojourner Truth: A Northern Slave.* Sojourner went on to fight for women's rights. At the age of 70, Sojourner was asked by President Andrew Johnson to work at the Freedmen's Hospital, and she also lived and was active in the Freedmen's Village on Robert E. Lee's abandoned plantation in Arlington, Virginia. The plight of newly freed people continued to plague her, and she sought to have government land in the west set aside for African Americans. Sojourner Truth died on November 26, 1883, in Battle Creek, Michigan, at the age of 86.

READ ABOUT HER

◆ *Sojourner Truth and the Struggle for Freedom* by Edward Beecher Claflin (Barron's Educational Series, 1987)

◆ *Walking the Road to Freedom: A Story About Sojourner Truth* by Jeri Ferris (Lerner, 1989)

◆ *Sojourner Truth: Ain't I a Woman?* by Patricia C. McKissack and Frederick McKissack (Scholastic, 1992)

TALK ABOUT HER

A Book of Life: Sojourner Truth kept a "Book of Life," a scrapbook/autograph book. Abraham Lincoln signed it, and so did Ulysses S. Grant. Ask students to think about what they would include in their own books. Suggest that they start a classroom "Book of Life." Students can discuss which events in their own lives, in and out of school, they would like to include. They may want to keep track of local, national, and world events, too. Suggest that they make a list of people they admire. Students can then write letters to them.

From Sojourner Truth to Rosa Parks: Sojourner Truth tried to board a street car in Washington, D.C., with Laura Haviland, a friend who was white. The conductor didn't know that the two women were together. He told Sojourner to stand aside and let the "lady" (Haviland) get on board. When Sojourner protested that she was a lady, too, the conductor shoved her and broke her collarbone. Sojourner sued and won. Nearly 100 years later, a driver tried to force Rosa Parks off a bus. What else do students know about Rosa Parks and the result of her refusal? Discuss the two events with students, and ask them to draw parallels between the two women.

WRITE ABOUT HER

A Woman's Work: Women also were treated unfairly during the 19th century. They weren't allowed to vote or own property, and were paid far less for doing the same work as men. Encourage students to investigate the women's suffrage and feminist movements. Ask them to conduct research to compare the differences between women who lived during the 19th century with women today. Explore the types of jobs women hold today that they couldn't in the past.

Freedmen's Bureaus and Villages: After President Lincoln signed the Emancipation Proclamation in 1863, he set up the Freedmen's Bureau and Freedman's Villages in Arlington, Virginia. Have students investigate these institutions. Ask them to make a model of a Freedman's Village, or describe a typical day at the Freedman's Bureau in a progress report to the President.

HARRIET TUBMAN
North to Freedom

By Tonya Leslie

CHARACTERS (in order of appearance):

ANGELA PATTERSON: 12-year-old girl

SID PATTERSON: Angela's grandfather

MARY: Mistress of a plantation in Maryland

JACK: Mary's husband

LAWYER

HARRIET TUBMAN

WOMAN

SUZANNE BANKS: Angela's great-great-grandmother

BENJAMIN: Harriet's brother (nonspeaking role)

JOHN: Harriet's brother (nonspeaking role)

WILLIAM HENRY: Harriet's brother (nonspeaking role)

BEN ROSS: Harriet's father

ACT 1

SCENE 1: Present day. Angela's home.

ANGELA: Today in class we learned about Harriet Tubman. She led hundreds of people out of slavery.

SID: *(pretending to be surprised)* Did she now? How'd she go about doing that?

ANGELA: There was this trail that went from South to North. It was called the Underground Railroad. Harriet Tubman was like a conductor on the railroad. She'd take a group of people up north, and then turn right around and head south again to pick up more.

SID: *(still acting surprised)* Do tell—the Underground Railroad? I believe I've heard something about that.

ANGELA: *(catching on)* Hey! You're pretty old. Maybe you knew her?

SID: *(laughing)* Pretty old, but not *that* old! *(getting serious)* Someone in our family did know her, though.

ANGELA: Who?!

SID: My great-grandmother—your great-great-grandmother—Suzanne Banks. My grandmother told me how Suzanne met Harriet Tubman.

ANGELA: Tell me!

SID: First, you have to promise to tell your children and grandchildren, too.

ANGELA: No problem, I love telling stories.

SID: Okay—then here goes. We'll start with Harriet Tubman. This is a story about her when she was just a little girl. She was born on a plantation owned by a man named Brodas. When she was just five years old, Brodas hired her out to one of his neighbors. He made Harriet sleep on the floor, and she didn't have anything to eat but table scraps. The man made her check his muskrat traps. You ever have to check on a muskrat trap? No? For Harriet, it meant having to wade barefoot in a freezing cold river. She got sick, and the man sent her back to Brodas.

SCENE 2: About the year 1827. Kitchen of a plantation in Maryland. Mary, the mistress of the plantation, is holding her baby and arguing with her husband. Harriet is standing near the kitchen table where a bowl filled with sugar cubes sits.

SID: *(from the side)* Brodas hired Harriet out again when she was seven years old. The woman of the plantation needed help taking care of her baby.

MARY: I don't care if Brodas came in here and dumped a sack full of pure gold on that kitchen table, I don't want to sell him that land!

JACK: We need the money—

MARY: If we need money, then stop buying horses!

(Hungry, Harriet looks longingly at the sugar. She finally edges toward the table and reaches out for the bowl.)

JACK: We need horses almost as—

MARY: You little—steal from me, will you? You'll be sorry you even *looked* at that piece of sugar!

(Harriet runs out the door, and Mary chases her.)

SID: *(from the side)* Harriet found a big, old pigpen and hid there. She stayed there for five days until she got so hungry she had to go back. The mistress of the plantation sent Harriet back to Brodas.

SCENE 1: Present day. Angela's home

ANGELA: So much happened to her, and she was still a little girl. How long was it until she ran away?

SID: Harriet Tubman must have been about 30 years old when she escaped. She was a married woman by then. But before then, she found out she'd been cheated out of her freedom.

ANGELA: Cheated?! How?

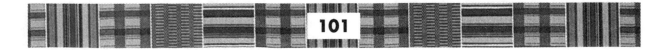

SID: I told you that Harriet got married—she married a free man named John Tubman.

ANGELA: If her husband was free, wouldn't that mean that Harriet was free, too?

SID: That's not the way things worked. John Tubman's parents got their freedom before he was born, so that meant he wasn't born into slavery. Harriet was.

ANGELA: Is that how she was cheated out of her freedom?

SID: No, that's another story. Her mother was called Old Rit. Old Rit said she'd been promised her freedom by her "owner." Harriet decided to go to a lawyer.

SCENE 2: 1845. A lawyer's office in Maryland.

LAWYER: The will is very clear. It states that your mother should have won her freedom when she turned 45. Legally, that means that you should be free, too.

HARRIET: Then how come she was sold when that man died? Didn't anybody read his will? I bet they sure divided up his land and his money.

LAWYER: Unfortunately, there's nothing we can do for you or your mother now.

HARRIET: *(in amazement)* Why not? You've got a piece of paper that says my mother and I are free. What else do we need?

LAWYER: It's not that simple. Too much time has gone by. You and your mother have always lived as slaves. There's no judge, South or North, who would give either one of you your freedom. I'm sorry. We're just too late.

HARRIET: Too late? Too late? Show me the law that says I lose because somebody else didn't pay attention to the law. *(getting up to leave the office)* I guess if y'all can bend the law, I can, too.

LAWYER: *(upset)* Please, Harriet, don't do anything . . .

HARRIET: I should be free, shouldn't I?

LAWYER: Yes, but ...

HARRIET: Then I won't be doing anything wrong.

ACT 3

SCENE 1: Present day. Angela's home.

SID: Only a few days after that meeting, Harriet found out that she was being sold. She made up her mind right then to escape by herself.

ANGELA: All by herself? Didn't her husband want to go with her? Didn't she have any family around that she could go with?

SID: John Tubman was free. He didn't want to go up north. He was so much against it that he told Harriet he'd turn her in if she tried to run away. Still, she tried to escape a couple of times with her two brothers, but they always got scared. They always made Harriet turn back.

ANGELA: Wasn't Harriet scared to go off all by herself?

SID: No. Harriet was used to the woods. Her father used to take her there when she was little. He told her what berries were safe to eat and how to find her way by following the North Star.

SCENE 2: 1849. Midnight. Tired and hungry, Harriet cautiously approaches a house in the woods.

HARRIET: I hope everybody was right. If this woman turns me in instead of helping me . . .

(She takes a deep breath and knocks on the door. A white woman opens the door. She doesn't seem surprised to see Harriet.)

WOMAN: Yes? How can I help you?

HARRIET: Please ma'am, I saw your hens and thought you might have a few eggs for sale. I have money to pay you. *(hesitating, then taking a chance)* I'm hungry, and I have a long trip ahead of me.

WOMAN: I can spare an egg or two. Please, come in, eat and rest a while.

(Harriet enters the woman's house.)

HARRIET: I've heard you're a very kind woman. You help people.

WOMAN: I do what I can. Sit down while I fix you some food. *(Before going out, the woman places two hand-drawn maps beside Harriet.)* Study these. Remember the houses I've marked. These are folks who can help you on your way north.

HARRIET: *(relieved)* It's true. You *are* a very kind woman.

SCENE 1: Present day.

ANGELA: Okay, so Harriet made it up North. How did she meet great-great-grandmother Suzanne Banks?

SID: She did make it to the north, but she made a promise to herself to help others escape. She rescued many people from slavery, including most of her own family—and Suzanne Banks. As news of Harriet's successes spread, her trips became more and more dangerous. The plantation owners put up a $10,000 reward for her capture.

ANGELA: *(impatiently)* What about Suzanne Banks?

SCENE 2: Late on Christmas Eve 1854. A group of people, including Harriet Tubman wait inside an old building on a plantation.

SID: *(from the side)* It's Christmas Eve. Harriet is in charge of more "passengers"—three of them are her brothers, and one is Suzanne Banks. They're to be "sold south" on the day after Christmas.

SUZANNE: *(anxiously)* Is this a good idea? I don't think this is a good idea.

HARRIET: Sshh! We won't be here for long. Benjy, take John and William Henry with you. Don't let Mama see you. Don't let her know we're out here. Just get Daddy out here.

(The three brothers disappear.)

SUZANNE: I don't like this! If we get caught, do you know what'll happen to us?

HARRIET: Don't worry. I've made twenty trips, and I haven't lost anyone yet.

(The brothers return with their father, Ben Ross, who has a bandanna tied over his eyes so he can't see.)

HARRIET: Daddy, it's me. It's Harriet.

(They hug for a very long time.)

BEN ROSS: How ya doing, baby? Everybody's always talking about you.

HARRIET: I'm taking the boys up North with me. Then I'll come back for you.

BEN ROSS: *(shaking his head)* We're too old to travel, and too old to sell. Old Rit and I are safe right where we are. Good-bye, boys. Get word to us, if you can.

(The brothers hug their father.)

HARRIET: We've got to go now. Wait about five minutes if you can, Daddy, and then take off the bandanna. *(She embraces her father.)* Tell Mama I love her.

SCENE 3: Present day. Angela's home.

SID: Ben Ross was questioned about his sons' disappearance, but he was a well-trusted man. He was able to say that he hadn't seen his children—and he hadn't. Three years later, Harriet managed to help her parents escape to the North.

ANGELA: That's it? I hate to say it, but great-great-grandmother Suzanne Banks doesn't sound like much of a hero.

SID: She was in her own way. She said herself that she started the trip as a girl and ended it as a woman.

ANGELA: How *long* did that trip take?

SID: *(laughing)* She meant she grew up on that trip. She saw how Harriet Tubman not only led the way, finding them food and shelter, but also keeping up their spirits when they were tired and scared. Suzanne Banks always said Harriet Tubman taught her how to be brave.

THE END

Teacher's Guide
HARRIET TUBMAN

QUOTES

There was one of two things I had a right to, liberty or death; if I could not have one, I would have the other; for no man should take me alive; I should fight for my liberty as long as my strength lasted, and when the time came for me to go, the Lord would let them take me.

I never ran my train off the track, and I never lost a passenger.

BIOGRAPHY

Harriet Tubman was born on the Brodas plantation in Dorchester County, Maryland, probably around 1820. Her parents, Ben Ross and Harriet Green (also known as Old Rit), had both been born in Africa but were transported to the United States to work as slaves. By the age of five, Harriet was hired out as a worker by Brodas. In 1835, while refusing to help hold down a man running away from slavery, fifteen-year-old Harriet was accidentally hit in the head with a two-pound weight. Never treated by a doctor, the injury caused her sleeping fits throughout her life.

In 1844 Harriet married John Tubman, a free black man. In 1849, after learning that she was to be "sold South," Harriet made her escape to Pennsylvania alone. Within a year of her escape she began the task of freeing her family. By 1857, after 19 trips on the Underground Railroad, Harriet Tubman had not only freed most of her family including her two aging parents, but also about 300 other people. Her efforts earned her the nickname of Moses.

Harriet Tubman's work didn't end with the Underground Railroad. She also served in the Civil War as a spy and a nurse, and continued to be a freedom fighter until she died in 1913 at the age of 92.

READ ABOUT HER

 ◆ *Harriet Tubman* by Terry Bisson (Chelsea House, 1991)

 ◆ *Get on Board: The Story of the Underground Railroad* by Jim Haskins (Scholastic, 1994)

 ◆ *Freedom Train: The Story of Harriet Tubman* by Dorothy Sterling (Scholastic, 1987)

TALK ABOUT HER

It's Not Easy to Say Good-bye: Harriet Tubman married a free black man who didn't want her to run away. Harriet's own brothers made a few attempts to escape but turned back. Hold a classroom discussion about the reasons for and against escaping to the North. Ask students to consider why some people might be afraid to run away, or might not want to escape to the North.

Creative Codes: Like most slaves, Harriet Tubman wasn't given the opportunity to learn how to read or write. Detailed coded messages were often passed from one person to the next in many different ways. Talk about the reasons why coded messages were so important in providing information among enslaved people. Ask students to think of ways in which they could communicate secretly among themselves without using the written word.

WRITE ABOUT HER

All Aboard!: Where was the starting point of the Underground Railroad? Where did it end? Guide students in researching the details of the Underground Railroad from its route, to passwords, way stations, number of passengers, and dates of operation. Then ask them to plan modern-day trips along the same route. Acting as tour guides, students can make up itineraries incorporating their research and contrasting the present-day locales to their appearances in the 1800s.

Songs of the South: According to one story, Harriet Tubman sang the following spiritual underneath the kitchen window where her sister worked.

> I'll meet you in the morning,
> When I reach the Promised Land,
> On the other side of Jordan,
> For I'm bound for the Promised Land.

The next day, Harriet left for the North. Encourage students to find out more about the history and role of spirituals in the South. They can select their own favorite songs to include in a classroom songbook. Students may wish to perform the spirituals themselves.

IDA B. WELLS-BARNETT
Writing Against Injustice

By Shelli Milks

CHARACTERS (in order of appearance):

NARRATOR

FAMILY FRIENDS 1-5

IDA B. WELLS-BARNETT

PEGGY: Ida's grandmother

EUGENIA: Ida's younger sister

DR. GRAY: Physician in Holly Springs, Mississippi

CONDUCTOR

PASSENGERS 1 AND 2

PORTER

REVEREND NIGHTINGALE: Co-owner of the *Free Speech and Headlight*

JOHN FLEMING: Co-owner of the *Free Speech and Headlight*

SUPERINTENDENT OF MEMPHIS SCHOOLS

ACT 1

SCENE 1: Fall of 1878. At a farm in Mississippi.

NARRATOR: Ida Wells just turned 16. She was visiting her grandmother, Peggy, who owned a farm in Mississippi. Her mother, Elizabeth, and her father, Jim, stayed at home with the rest of their children. Ida missed her family, but wasn't worried when she didn't hear from them. Mail delivery to Peggy's farm was slow. Then one day, three friends of her parents rode up to the front gate.

FRIEND 1: Ida! Ida Bell!

IDA: Oh, I'm so glad to see you all! How's my family?

FRIEND 2: Is your grandmother here, Ida?

IDA: She's inside. I'm so glad to see you, I've forgotten my manners. Please, come on in. And Baby Stanley? Do you know if he's walking yet? How are the boys? What about Annie and Lily? And Eugenia? How's Eugenia? *(calling out)* Grandmother! Company's come!

FRIEND 3: Ida, slow down. The yellow jack epidemic's hit Holly Springs hard.

IDA: We heard about it. We thought sure Mother and Father must have taken everyone to Aunt Belle's . . .

PEGGY: *(hurrying in)* Aren't we glad to see you all! We've been hoping to get some news from Holly Springs.

FRIEND 1: I'm afraid the news isn't good.

FRIEND 2: Why don't you two sit down?

IDA: Someone's caught the fever, haven't they?

FRIEND 3: It's your parents, Ida, and little Stanley.

IDA: I've got to get home right away. They'll need somebody to take care of them.

FRIEND 3: I'm sorry, Ida. It's too late. They're gone.

PEGGY: Gone? Where?

FRIEND 1: Give Ida the letter. Let her read it.

(Friend 2 hands a letter to Ida.)

IDA *(reading aloud):* "Jim and Lizzie Wells—have both died of the fever within twenty-four hours of each other. The children are all at home and the Howard Association has put a woman there to take care of them. Send word to Ida." *(Upset, puts the letter down)* I've got to go back right away.

PEGGY: No! You can't go back. What if *you* get sick?

IDA: I'm the oldest. My brothers and sisters need me right now.

PEGGY: You're no more than a child yourself. You're not done with school yet. You can't take care of five children all by yourself. Wait until the epidemic's over.

IDA: No. I have to go home. I can't wait.

SCENE 2: A few days later. At the Wells home in Holly Springs, Mississippi.

NARRATOR: Ida took the train home. Her brothers and sisters had recovered, but they were sad and frightened. Dr. Gray, who treated her parents, came by the house to tell Ida about what happened. Family friends came by, too, with a plan.

EUGENIA: They turned the courthouse into a hospital, and Daddy was there all day long, helping out. Then Mama got sick . . .

DR. GRAY: He took care of your mother, and all your brothers and sisters when they came down with the fever. It's no surprise he caught it himself. Your father was a brave and generous man.

EUGENIA: Dr. Gray's been watching over us since then.

DR. GRAY: Your father gave me $300 to hold for you, Miss Wells. If you need anything at all, you let me know.

FRIEND 1: Don't worry, Doctor. We've decided what to do.

FRIEND 2: Ida, come over here and sit down.

FRIEND 3: I'm going to take the boys. James and George will be my apprentices. They'll live and work with me.

FRIEND 4: I'll take Annie.

FRIEND 5: I'll take Lily.

EUGENIA: What about me? Where will I go? I'm crippled! If no one wants me, I'll go to the poor house!

IDA: No, you won't. Nobody's going anywhere. We're all staying here in this house. We own it. We have some money.

FRIEND 2: That money won't last forever, Ida. Be realistic.

IDA: Believe me, I am. I have a good education. I'll take the teaching exam. If I pass, I can teach at a country school.

FRIEND 3: Stop being so stubborn. Listen to our advice.

IDA: I'm not being stubborn. I'm being practical. We appreciate what you've done for us. I'll always *listen* to your advice, but I can't promise that I'll take it.

NARRATOR: Ida passed the test and became a schoolteacher. For a while, Peggy moved to Holly Springs and watched over the other children during the week. On weekdays, Ida taught and stayed in the homes of her students. On weekends, she returned to Holly Springs to take care of her family. Unfortunately, Peggy had to return to her farm because of poor health. The children's aunts came up with an idea. Aunt Belle offered Eugenia and the boys a home. Annie and Lily would live with Aunt Fanny. Ida reluctantly accepted their offer.

ACT 2

SCENE: May 4, 1884. On a train outside of Memphis, Tennessee.

NARRATOR: Ida took a teaching job in Woodstock, Tennessee. The small community was ten miles away from Memphis. She lived in Memphis and traveled by train to Woodstock. During the summers, Ida went to college. In her diary, she wrote about becoming a novelist or an actress. An event in 1884 led her in

another direction. One day, Ida boarded the train for Woodstock. She sat in the car called the ladies' coach—where she always sat.

CONDUCTOR: Tickets! Tickets, please!

IDA: Here you are, sir.

CONDUCTOR: I can't accept this ticket—not for this car. You have to move to the back of the train. That's where the car for blacks and smokers is.

IDA: I beg your pardon? I always sit in this car. I've done so every day for years.

CONDUCTOR: These cars are segregated. This is a car for white ladies only. That's the way it is. I don't make the laws. You'll have to leave.

IDA: I will not leave.

PASSENGER 1: Conductor, you must remove her!

PASSENGER 2: Please do, sir! Whites should not have to sit with blacks!

CONDUCTOR: *(grabbing Ida's arm)* You're upsetting the other passengers. Come along and don't cause any trouble.

IDA: I'm not going anywhere. Please, let go of me.

CONDUCTOR: That's it! *(He tries to pull Ida out of her seat.)* Help! I need a porter!

PORTER: *(rushing into the car)* What's going on?

CONDUCTOR: This woman's causing trouble. If she won't go willingly, we'll have to *drag* her to the car for blacks!

(The train pulls into the next station and stops.)

IDA: Don't worry, gentlemen. You don't have to drag me into the smokers' car. I'd rather walk than ride this train.

(The passengers applaud as Ida leaves the train.)

PASSENGER 1: Next time, go to the car where you belong!

IDA: *(watching the train pull out of the station)* They haven't heard the last of me.

NARRATOR: Ida hired a lawyer and sued the railroad. Her case was tried before Judge J.O. Pierce, a former Union officer, and she was awarded $500 in damages. Unfortunately, the state supreme court later decided *against* Ida. Now, she not only had to pay damages, but large court costs, as well.

SCENE 1: 1889. Newspaper offices of the *Free Speech and Headlight* in Memphis, Tennessee.

NARRATOR: The editor of *The Living Way*, a publication for a black church, asked Ida to write a story about her case. Response to her article was so good that she became a full-time columnist for the publication. Ida continued to teach as she wrote under the pen name of Iola. Other newspapers ran her columns, too. Iola became known for writing what was on her mind. She wasn't afraid to criticize whites or blacks. Ida loved writing, but she had other plans, too.

REVEREND NIGHTINGALE: I hope your news is good? Have you accepted our offer? Will you be a columnist for the *Free Speech and Headlight?*

IDA: I have an offer of my own to make.

JOHN FLEMING: More money?

REVEREND NIGHTINGALE: You can write whatever you want. We won't—

IDA: I'd like to be more than a columnist. I want to buy into your newspaper.

JOHN FLEMING: You want to own part of the newspaper?

IDA: That's right. I'd like to be your partner *and* your new columnist. If I buy a third of the newspaper, we three would be equal partners. I like the sound of that!

REVEREND NIGHTINGALE: Do you have the money?

IDA: Don't worry. I'll find it.

SCENE 2: Fall 1890. Inside a Memphis school office.

NARRATOR: Although Ida became a partner in the *Free Speech and Headlight*, she continued to teach. Her editorials in the newspaper angered many people. Sometimes Ida paid a high price for her beliefs.

IDA: Where will I be teaching this fall?

SUPERINTENDENT: Well . . . you won't. The school board voted against hiring you again.

IDA: Why?!

SUPERINTENDENT: You seem to enjoy writing so much. . .

IDA: Is that what this is about? My editorials? You know what I wrote is true. Black schoolchildren don't have enough books or supplies. They don't have decent school buildings. They don't get the best teachers.

SUPERINTENDENT: Exactly. It's not your writing we have problems with. It's your teaching. We're giving your job to someone better.

IDA: I've been teaching for over 12 years, and I've never received a complaint. I've received plenty of complaints about what I write in my columns and editorials. You're firing me because I told the truth about the kind of education black children are getting.

SUPERINTENDENT: I'm in charge of the schools here. And I'm telling you that black children are getting the education they deserve. And I'm also telling you that you're fired.

IDA: In that case, I'll have more time to write. Keep your eye on the editorial page, Superintendent.

NARRATOR: Nothing kept Ida B. Wells from speaking out and writing about the injustices she saw. She also took action. Wells was the first woman in Chicago to be appointed as a probation officer. In 1929, at the age of 67, she ran for the state senate in Illinois. Ida wasn't elected, but her voice was heard. . .loud and clear.

THE END

Teacher's Guide
IDA B. WELLS-BARNETT

QUOTES

On her trip to Great Britain in 1894:
It was such an absolutely new thing to be permitted for once to associate with human beings who pay tribute to what they believe one possesses in the way of qualities of mind and heart, rather than the color of the skin.

I wrote in a plain, common-sense way on the things which concerned our people.

Let your songs be songs of faith and hope.

BIOGRAPHY

Ida Bell Wells was born into slavery on July 16, 1862, in Holly Springs, Mississippi. Both of her parents died in the yellow fever epidemic which swept the South in 1878. As a result, Ida quit school and assumed responsibility for her five brothers and sisters. For a year, she taught at a country school during the week while her grandmother looked after the family. Ida returned home on the weekends.

Ida's first political action came in 1884 when she was 22. She sued the Chesapeake and Ohio Railroad for discrimination after she was forcibly removed from her seat. Ida wrote about the incident in a publication directed to the African-American population, creating her reputation as an activist. Using the pen name of Iola, she chronicled the injustices against African Americans and women. Journalism became Ida's full-time career after she was fired from her teaching position for writing editorials critical of the Memphis school system's treatment of black children.

In 1895, Ida B. Wells married Ferdinand Barnett. They had four children. She is revered for many accomplishments: crusading against lynching, investigating race riots, founding the black women's club movement, and advocating women's suffrage. Ida B. Wells-Barnett was also one of the first African-American women to run for public office. She ran unsuccessfully for the Illinois state senate in 1930—at the age of 67! Ida also participated in the founding of the National Association for the Advancement of Colored People (NAACP).

READ ABOUT HER

* *Ida B. Wells-Barnett and the Antilynching Crusade* by Suzanne Freedman (The Millbrook Press, 1994)
* *Ida Wells-Barnett* by Steve Klots (Chelsea House, 1995)
* *The Memphis Diary of Ida B. Wells* edited by Miriam Decosta-Willis (Beacon Press, 1995)

TALK ABOUT HER

What's the Scoop?: Journalism has changed since Ida B. Wells-Barnett took up her pen. Open a discussion about the different forms of journalism today and the role of journalism in students' lives. Introduce these and other questions: What purpose does journalism serve? What might our country be like without a free press? Is it still possible for people to fight causes using written or spoken words?

Righting Wrongs: Ida used the legal system and the media to redress wrongs. Her strong stands on issues often upset people. What kinds of injustice do your students see in the world? What do they think might be done about correcting them? What if they were in danger of losing friends because of their stands on the issues? Would they continue to fight, compromise, or back down?

WRITE ABOUT HER

Read All About It!: Ida began her journalism career by writing a story about her own experiences. Let students establish their own journalistic careers by creating a classroom newspaper. They may wish to focus on classroom events only, or expand coverage to include their entire school or community. Before students begin, bring in several newspapers for them to study. Their paper should include different sections such as news, editorials, lifestyles, and sports sections.

Vote for Ida B. Wells-Barnett!: As an independent candidate, Wells-Barnett ran for the Illinois state senate. Assign students the task of heading her campaign. Have them come up with a campaign slogan and design buttons and bumper stickers. Students should also prepare a press kit containing her biography and stands on issues. You also may wish to let students hold a debate and role play Ida and the two other candidates who ran for the senate seat.

PHILLIS WHEATLEY
A Poetic Voice

By Egypt Freeman

CHARACTERS (in order of appearance):

NARRATORS 1 AND 2

SUSANNAH WHEATLEY: Phillis's mistress

JOHN WHEATLEY: Susannah's husband

PHILLIS WHEATLEY

MARY: Susannah and John's daughter

SOCIETY WOMEN 1 AND 2

EUNICE FITCH: Boston woman

MISS FITCH: Eunice's daughter

NATHANIEL WHEATLEY: Susannah and John's son

EARL OF DARTMOUTH: British man sympathetic to the Colonies

MESSENGER

GEORGE WASHINGTON: Commander-and-Chief during the Revolutionary war, and first President of the United States

ACT 1

SCENE: 1761. In the Boston home of John and Susannah Wheatley.

NARRATOR 1: Phillis Wheatley was kidnapped from her West African home by slave traders in 1761 and was taken to Boston, Massachusetts, on board the slave ship *Phillis*. She was seven years old. After eight months at sea, Phillis was very tired and sick.

NARRATOR 2: Susannah Wheatley went to the dock where the newly arrived Africans were to be auctioned off to the highest bidders. Susannah wanted to purchase a young and healthy girl to be a servant. Although Phillis wasn't as strong as Susannah would have liked, there was something special about the young girl that attracted Susannah's attention, so she bought her.

SUSANNAH: John, have you noticed how smart Phillis is?

JOHN: I don't know. I haven't thought much about it.

SUSANNAH: She's only been here for a few months, but she already speaks English better than some people we know.

JOHN: Let's hope her being smart doesn't work against us. We need a servant, not a girl who's too smart to do her work.

SUSANNAH: Nonsense. How can she do what we ask unless she understands us? Phillis, come here child. Show Master Wheatley what you showed me the other day.

PHILLIS: Yes ma'am.

(Using a piece of charcoal, she writes her name on a board.)

JOHN: She can write her name? I don't believe it! Phillis, who taught you to do that?

PHILLIS: No one sir. I taught myself.

JOHN: Tell the truth now, Phillis. Mary showed you that trick, didn't she?

PHILLIS: No, sir, I . . .

JOHN: Mary! Come in here!

(Mary hurries in.)

MARY: What is it? What's the matter?

JOHN: How long did it take you to teach Phillis this little trick?

MARY: *(looking astonished)* Phillis, did you write this?

PHILLIS: Yes, miss, I . . .

JOHN: *(laughing)* Mary, did you really think you could fool me?

MARY: I taught her a few letters, but I never showed her how to write her name. Phillis did that on her own.

JOHN: *(looking concerned)* Thank you, Phillis that will be all. Go help with the laundry. *(Phillis leaves the room.)* Susannah, it's dangerous for us to encourage the girl to read and write. That goes for you too, Mary. It won't do her any good as a slave.

SUSANNAH: What right have we to put out the desire for education that apparently burns inside the girl? It's our Christian duty to help Phillis develop whatever talent is inside of her.

JOHN: What about the other slaves? If they should want to learn too, are we to teach them, as well?

SUSANNAH: Phillis is different. I knew from the moment I saw her step off that wretched ship that she was a miracle sent to us. We must do all we can for her.

JOHN: It's a dangerous game to educate slaves, but . . . suppose Mary works a little with Phillis to help her with her studies?

MARY: I could help her in the afternoons, right after lunch.

JOHN: A little, I said. Don't get carried away.

SUSANNAH: Splendid John! Mary can start this afternoon.

JOHN: Here. *(He hands his daughter the book he's been reading)* I'll even donate this book of poetry to the cause.

NARRATOR 1: The next day, Mary began teaching Phillis how to read and write—a luxury not only for those who were enslaved, but also for many of the white colonists. Not all of them could read or write either.

NARRATOR 2: The Wheatleys treated Phillis as if she were their own daughter, which proved to be both good and bad. While it freed her to develop her artistic talent, it also separated her from the black community. The Wheatleys didn't allow Phillis to socialize with the other slaves.

ACT 2

SCENE: 1772. In the house of Timothy Fitch, the owner of the ship called the Phillis.

NARRATOR 1: Throughout Phillis's childhood and adolescence, she showed an extraordinary talent for poetry. She was called on to recite her poetry at the homes of some of the wealthiest and most influential people of Boston society.

NARRATOR 2: One of those homes belonged to Timothy Fitch, the owner of the slave ship *Phillis*. His wife Eunice invited Phillis to tea one day.

PHILLIS: *(reciting)*

> What sorrows labour in my parent's breast?
> Steeled was that soul and by no misery moved,
> That from a father seized his babe beloved:
> Such, such my case. And can I then but pray
> Others may never feel tyrannic sway?

SUSANNAH: *(beginning to clap)* Her newest poem. Isn't it moving? She wrote it for the Earl of Dartmouth.

SOCIETY WOMAN 1: He's British. What do they understand about "tyrannic sway?" Uh-oh, look at Eunice Fitch. I think it's just dawned on her what the girl meant in her poem.

SOCIETY WOMAN 2: If it weren't for Timothy Fitch, Phillis would still be living in Africa. She certainly wouldn't be writing poetry.

EUNICE: *(going up to Phillis)* That was lovely, Phillis. Please sit with us and have some tea.

PHILLIS: Thank you.

MISS FITCH: There's so much *feeling* in the poem. Most poets don't put themselves in their work. *(sitting beside Phillis)* You know, I can always remember your name. My father's boat is named the *Phillis*.

(There is an uncomfortable silence. The Society Woman look meaningfully at one other.)

SUSANNAH: Phillis knows, dear. She knows your father's boat very well. She spent a good deal of time on it. In fact, when she arrived in America, she was even *named* after it.

MISS FITCH: I've only been on board the boat when it's docked in the harbor. I've never gotten to sail on it.

PHILLIS: I don't think you would enjoy sailing on the *Phillis*.

MISS FITCH: Really? I'm a good sailor. I never get seasick or anything . . .

EUNICE: *(interrupting her daughter)* Do you take milk in your tea, Phillis?

SOCIETY WOMAN 1: Doesn't she *know* what her father brings in on that ship?

SOCIETY WOMAN 2: But imagine growing up in Africa, with no knowledge of the English language! I still say Timothy Fitch is the one who's made that girl a poet—not Susannah Wheatley.

SCENE 2: 1773. A drawing room in London.

NARRATOR 1: After getting many of Phillis's poems published in various newspapers, Susannah Wheatley wanted to publish a book of her poetry. Unable to find anyone in America willing to publish a book of poetry written by a slave, Susannah finally found a printer in London who agreed to do it.

NARRATOR 2: Soon Phillis found herself sailing for London. Her health was poor, and the doctors felt a sea voyage would help. Susannah and John Wheatleys' son Nathaniel had business in London and traveled with Phillis. Thanks to Susannah Wheatley, word of Phillis's talent had spread. She was a big hit in London.

NATHANIEL: I wish mother were here to see this.

PHILLIS: So do I. I think she would have enjoyed meeting Mr. Benjamin Franklin. He has so many interests . . . science and philosophy. He says Mistress Wheatley has chosen a good printer to do my book.

NATHANIEL: I'm very curious about meeting King George. He hasn't treated Boston very well, or the rest of the colonies.

PHILLIS: The Earl of Dartmouth has sent him some of my poems. Maybe they'll help the king see how we feel about our freedom.

EARL OF DARTMOUTH: *(walking up to Phillis and Nathaniel)* Did I hear my name?

PHILLIS: We were just talking about meeting the king, and missing Mrs. Wheatley.

EARL OF DARTMOUTH: I've written to her just today, telling her what a success you're having here in London. I hope you'll stay here for a good long while. There are so many people I want you to meet.

PHILLIS: I love it here. I love talking to people and hearing new ideas. I love Boston, too, but it's different here.

MESSENGER *(handing an envelope to Nathaniel):* Beg your pardon, sir. This just came for you.

(Nathaniel opens the envelope and reads the letter inside.)

PHILLIS: What is it? Is it bad news?

NATHANIEL: It's mother. She's taken ill.

PHILLIS: I must go back.

EARL OF DARTMOUTH: But surely it's not that serious. You haven't met the king yet.

PHILLIS: No. She's sick. She needs me.

NATHANIEL: Stay, Phillis. I'll go back. If it's really serious, I'll let you know. You may not have an opportunity like this again.

PHILLIS: I can't stay here knowing that your mother is ill. I'll be ready to leave in the morning.

NARRATOR 1: Phillis's book, *Poems on Various Subjects, Religious and Moral*, appeared in September of 1773. It received high praise. Some British critics, however, attacked the Wheatleys for not freeing Phillis.

NARRATOR 2: Soon afterward, Susannah Wheatley gave Phillis her freedom. Phillis continued to live with the Wheatleys and to care for Susannah, but she had to earn her own living. Susannah Wheatley died on March 3, 1774. With this loss, Phillis truly was on her own. There was more change ahead. That summer, the British threw up a blockade around Boston Harbor. Revolution was in the air.

ACT 3

SCENE: March 1776. George Washington's army camp in Cambridge, Massachusetts.

NARRATOR 1: Tension between the Colonies and Great Britain eventually led to war. The battle of Lexington and Concord on April 19, 1775 launched the American Revolution.

NARRATOR 2: Impressed with the leadership of General George Washington, Phillis wrote a poem for him entitled "To His Excellency General Washington." Impressed in turn by Phillis Wheatley, Washington invited her to visit him in Cambridge, Massachusetts.

WASHINGTON: Welcome to my headquarters, Miss Phillis.

PHILLIS: It's an honor for you to receive me, sir.

WASHINGTON: I must admit that when you sent me your poem last October, I was caught up in so much that I laid it aside and did not come across again it until recently. But I've memorized a portion of it:

> One century scarce perform'd its destined round,
> When Gallic powers Columbia's fury found;
> And so may you, whoever dares disgrace
> The land of freedom's heaven-defended race!

PHILLIS: *(continuing the verse)*

> Fix'd are the eyes of the nations on the scales,
> For in their hopes Columbia's arm prevails
> Anon Britannia droops the pensive head,
> While round increase the rising hills of dead.
> Ah! cruel blindness to Columbia's state!
> Lament thy thirst of boundless power too late.

WASHINGTON: Tell me, what inspires you to write such beautiful words?

PHILLIS: Life inspires me to write, sir. When I first began, it was because I had learned how to do it, how to read and write. But then I found myself compelled to use words to record these times in poetry.

WASHINGTON: Your poems are indeed a blessing and your talent a wondrous gift.

NARRATOR 1: But even meeting George Washington did not help Phillis regain the popularity and prosperity she had once enjoyed. She continued to publish poems in local newspapers. Although she had enough poems for a second book, Phillis was unable to find a publisher.

NARRATOR 2: After marrying John Peters, a struggling black businessman, on April 1, 1778, she had two children, both of whom died shortly after birth. Phillis Wheatley died in poverty on December 5, 1784. Today her talent has been rediscovered. We celebrate her as the first published African-American poet.

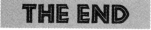

THE END

Teacher's Guide
PHILLIS WHEATLEY

QUOTES

In every human breast, God has implanted a principle, which we call love of freedom; it is impatient of oppression, and pants for deliverance.

On the death of Susannah Wheatley:
Let us imagine the loss of a parent, sister or brother. The tenderness of all these was united in her. I was a poor little outcast and stranger when she took me in; not only into her house, but I presently became a sharer in her most tender affections. I was treated by her more like her child than her servant.

BIOGRAPHY

Phillis Wheatley, born in approximately 1753, was the first African-American writer to be published. Kidnapped from her West African home at the age of seven by slave traders, she was brought to America and purchased by the prosperous Wheatley family of Boston. By the time she was nine, Phillis had mastered English and Latin, and had begun to write poetry. Her first poem was published when she was 14. During adolescence, Phillis became well-known for her poetry and visited the homes of the New England elite to recite her work.

Her only book, *Poems on Various Subjects, Religious and Moral*, was published in London in 1773 and brought her international acclaim. Granted her freedom just before the American Revolution began in 1775, Wheatley spent the rest of her life struggling for survival in a world more concerned with war than poetry. She entered a difficult marriage with John Peters. The couple had two children, neither of whom survived. Phillis Wheatley died penniless and alone on December 5, 1784, at the age of 31.

READ ABOUT HER

* *The Story of Phillis Wheatley: Poetess of the American Revolution* by Shirley Graham (Julian Messner, 1969)
* *Phillis Wheatley, Poet* by Merle Richmond (Chelsea House, 1988)
* *The Collected Works of Phillis Wheatley* edited by John C. Shields (Oxford University Press, 1988)

TALK ABOUT HER

A Member of the Family?: When Phillis Wheatley's book of poetry was published, the critics praised her work. They weren't so kind to Susannah Wheatley, though. Since Phillis still legally "belonged" to Susannah and John Wheatley, the critics felt Susannah's treatment of Phillis was hypocritical. But according to Phillis's own words, she was treated as a member of the Wheatley family. How do your students feels about the role of Susannah in Phillis's life? Did special treatment isolate Phillis from the black community without giving her true and full access to the privileges enjoyed by whites?

Voicing Concerns: Phillis Wheatley lived in a very turbulent time in American history. She wrote about the people and events she witnessed. Which current events most affect your students? If they could meet the President of the United States, what would they ask him to change or do? Guide them in verbally composing a class poem that reflects their concerns about the world in which they live. If students agree, send their poem to the White House.

WRITE ABOUT HER

A Hard Passage from Home: Phillis Wheatley was transported from her home in West Africa on the slave ship the *Phillis*, and was named after the ship. Present the following topics to your students to research: Phillis's home in West Africa (its people, history, traditions, government, and so on) or the slave trade (the conditions, route, points of origin, and destinations). Encourage students interested in the same topics to work in groups, and let them present their work to the rest of the class.

Inaugurating a New Morning: Phillis Wheatley wrote a poem for George Washington, who later became President of the United States. When Bill Clinton was inaugurated, he asked the poet Maya Angelou to write a poem for the event. Ask students to compare and contrast Phillis Wheatley's poem with Maya Angelou's. What does each poem say about the times in which it was written? What is their personal response to the poems? Have students wind up their reports with questions they would like to ask both poets about their lives and their work.

MALCOLM X
Born Too Late, Died Too Soon

By Justin Martin

CHARACTERS (in order of appearance):

NARRATOR

MALCOLM: At the ages of 4, 6, 13, and a young adult

PHILBERT: Malcolm's brother

EARL LITTLE: Malcolm's father

LOUISE LITTLE: Malcolm's mother

WILFRED: The Little's eldest child

HILDA: Malcolm's sister

REGINALD: Malcolm's brother

MR. HACKETT: Malcolm's teacher

SHORTY: Malcolm's friend in Harlem

RATMAN: Malcolm's friend in Harlem

"FINGERS" JONES: Malcolm's friend in Harlem

BIMBI: Inmate at Charlestown State Prison

PRISON GUARD

ELIJAH MUHAMMAD: Leader of the Nation of Islam

NATION OF ISLAM MEMBERS 1-5 (nonspeaking roles)

POLICE CAPTAIN

ACT 1: MALCOLM LITTLE

NARRATOR: Malcolm X was born in Omaha, Nebraska, on May 19, 1925. His name was originally Malcolm Little. His father was a travelling minister. What follows are a series of "snapshots" of early experiences that shaped Malcolm's view of the world.

SNAPSHOT 1: 1929. Outside the Little's burning house in Lansing, Michigan.

PHILBERT: Did they burn down our *whole* house?

EARL LITTLE: It looks that way.

HILDA: Are we going to have to move someplace new?

LOUISE LITTLE: We don't have a house anymore. We'll have to move.

REGINALD: What about my toys?

LOUISE LITTLE: We'll try to buy new ones when we can afford them.

WILFRED: Was it white folks that did this?

EARL LITTLE: Yes, son.

MALCOLM: Why, Daddy? Why did they burn down our house?

EARL LITTLE: They don't like the kind of work I do. They think I'm stirring up trouble.

SNAPSHOT 2: The middle of the night on September 28, 1931. Inside the Little's living room in Lansing. Malcolm is now six years old.

LOUISE LITTLE: *(letting out a long wail)* Oh, nooooo! Noooooooo!

(The Little children hurry into the room.)

HILDA: Mama, what's wrong?

LOUISE LITTLE: *(can barely speak)* Your father . . . he's, he's . . .

PHILBERT: What's happened? What's happened to Dad?

LOUISE LITTLE: He's dead. Your father's dead.

MALCOLM: What happened to Daddy?

LOUISE LITTLE: They murdered him. First, they burn down our house, but that's not good enough. *(She walks to the window and yells out into the night):* A good man is dead! A good black man is dead! I hope you're happy.

SNAPSHOT 3: West Junior High School in Mason, Michigan. Malcolm is 13 years old.

MR. HACKETT: Malcolm, tell me, what would you like to be when you grow up?

MALCOLM: A lawyer.

MR. HACKETT: *(laughing)* A lawyer? Malcolm, you're a smart kid, there's no doubt about it. But you have to be realistic. A lawyer *(shaking his head)*—that's just not a realistic goal for a Negro. You're good with your hands. Why don't you think about becoming a carpenter.

ACT 2: DETROIT RED

SCENE 1: 1940s. Late night inside a Harlem apartment.

NARRATOR: By his late teens, Malcolm was on his own and had moved to a place where he was better accepted—Harlem, a predominantly black neighborhood in New York City. He used all the latest, coolest slang of the day—"cats" and "daddy-o." To go along with his new identity, Malcolm had a new name—"Detroit Red"—"Detroit" because no one had ever heard of Lansing, Michigan, where he had come from, and "Red" because of his red hair.

MALCOLM: I spent all my money tonight. I don't have a nickel to my name. How am I supposed to impress my lady friends if I'm not wearing some sharp new threads next time I see one of them? I need some cash fast.

SHORTY: Don't look at me, Red. I'm two weeks late with the rent. The land-lord's about to run me out of my place.

RATMAN: You guys think you have problems. I've got a $50 gambling debt. If I don't pay One-Eyed Leroy by next Tuesday he says he's going to break my thumbs.

FINGERS: *(sarcastically)* Maybe we should get jobs. I'll go to the bank tomorrow and see if they need a new vice-president.

(Everyone laughs.)

SHORTY: Now, you're talking crazy stuff, Fingers. You know there ain't no decent jobs. Not for folks like us.

MALCOLM: Oh, don't be so sure. Listen up, cats, and I'll fill you in on a prime employment opportunity. I know of this couple down the street that's loaded. I say we drop by and tidy their place up. Pick up a few things, you know. A little cash here, a radio there.

FINGERS: House cleaning. Now that's my kind of work.

SHORTY: Let me get this straight, Detroit Red: We just walk in there and take their stuff?

MALCOLM: It's as simple as that, my man. I know the cat who works as their doorman, and he has a master key.

RATMAN: Yeah, but what if they're home?

MALCOLM: Don't sweat it. This doorman says they leave tomorrow for vacation. Two weeks. This cat says the Mrs. has got diamonds, emeralds, *and* rubies. It'll be easier than taking candy from a baby.

SHORTY: Detroit Red, you ever tried taking candy from a baby?

ACT 3: PRISONER #22843

SCENE: 1946. Mess hall of Charlestown State Prison in Boston.

Narrator: Being a "cool cat" didn't prove a good identity for Malcolm. In fact, it landed him in prison. In February of 1946, Malcolm just shy of his 21st birthday, was sentenced to ten years for armed robbery. Now he had a new identity: Prisoner #22843.

BIMBI: Do you think it's possible to be free even when you're in prison?

MALCOLM: That is the stupidest question I have ever heard.

BIMBI: C'mon, Malcolm, stop stuffing your face with mashed potatoes for a second and think about it.

MALCOLM: I don't want to think about it. I want to eat.

BIMBI: Then your mind really is in prison.

MALCOLM: Where else would it be? Look around. I see bars, I see guards, I see other prisoners. I don't know where you are, but I'm in prison.

BIMBI: Just because they have your body locked up doesn't mean they can control your mind. Your imagination is still free. Your mind can travel anywhere.

MALCOLM: If my mind could travel, first thing it would do is go to a restaurant and pick up some decent food.

BIMBI: You're clever, Malcolm. With the right training you could be a lawyer.

NARRATOR: That got Malcolm's attention. He began to pay attention to what Bimbi said. Soon Malcolm was reading great works by Harriet Beecher Stowe, Mahatma Gandhi, Socrates, and W.E.B. DuBois, learning all about his heritage, philosophy, and science. Around this time, Malcolm's brother Reginald visited him in prison. Just as Bimbi had introduced Malcolm to books, Reginald opened his brother's eyes to another world.

SCENE 2: In the prison visitors center.

REGINALD: Who do you think our ancestors were?

MALCOLM: Slaves, what else?

REGINALD: What were they *before* they were forced into slavery?

MALCOLM: (*shrugging*) I don't know—people in Africa.

REGINALD: Not just people in Africa, Malcolm. We're descended from ancient civilizations in Egypt and Ethiopia. Once, Egypt was as powerful a country as

the United States is today. Its king and queen were black; its richest merchants were black; its lawyers and scientists and teachers were black. Our ancestors even had their own religion. It's called Islam, and the followers of Islam are known as Muslims.

MALCOLM: Black lawyers *even*—looks like I was born in the wrong time and the wrong place.

REGINALD: It's not just ancient Egypt, Malcolm. I've joined the Nation of Islam, right here in the United States, right in Detroit. Our leader, the Honorable Elijah Muhammad, teaches us pride in being black and pride in our heritage.

PRISON GUARD: *(interrupting them)* Visiting time's over. Enough jabbering. You'll have to finish planning your escape next time.

REGINALD: *(to Malcolm as he's being led away by the guard)* Learn about Islam, Malcolm. It will make you free.

NARRATOR: Malcolm started writing letters to Elijah Muhammad to learn all about Islam. He began to pray to God, or Allah. In accordance with the beliefs of his new religion, Malcolm gave up smoking and stopped eating pork. Sure enough, the combination of reading books and finding a new religion made Malcolm feel free just as his friend Bimbi and his brother Reginald had predicted. Malcolm began to feel more free in prison than he had growing up in Michigan hanging out in Harlem.

ACT 4: MALCOLM X

SCENE 1: 1952. The living room of Elijah Muhammad's Chicago home.

NARRATOR: In 1952, at the age of 27, Malcolm was released from prison. He moved to Detroit where he lived with his brother Wilfred and spread the word about the Muslim faith. Soon, Malcolm had a chance to visit Elijah Muhammad in Chicago. He would always remember that first meeting as one of the most exciting events in his life.

ELIJAH MUHAMMAD: Sit down, Malcolm, sit down. Make yourself comfortable.

MALCOLM: Thank you, sir.

ELIJAH MUHAMMAD: You are recently out of prison. Certain people, of course, get to feeling very religious in prison. Once the bars are removed, they return to their old ways. From your letters, you strike me as a man who is serious in his resolve, a man who has no intention of returning to his former ways.

MALCOLM: No sir. From now on I want to devote my life to Islam.

ELIJAH MUHAMMAD: That's a noble mission. But believe me, your faith will be tested. Just remember: For every step you take towards Allah, he will take two steps toward you.

MALCOLM: That's a great comfort, sir.

ELIJAH MUHAMMAD: Remember, Malcolm, as a young man you are the Nation of Islam's greatest weapon. You understand other young people, you understand their temptations and their needs. If you show them that there is a better way, perhaps they will avoid making the mistakes that so many young black people are making today.

MALCOLM: I'll do my best, sir.

ELIJAH MUHAMMAD: Malcolm, I want to ask you a question. Where did you get your last name? Where is the name "Little" from?

MALCOLM: I don't know.

ELIJAH MUHAMMAD: Exactly. You don't know. Most likely it's the name that a slave master gave to one of your ancestors. But you have another more dignified name, an African name. Until you discover that name—the name that is rightfully yours — your last name shall be X. Now go forth and spread the faith, Brother Malcolm X.

MALCOLM: I will, sir. I will spread it far and wide.

NARRATOR: Many members of the Nation of Islam took the last name of X. There were Thomas X's, and James X's, and Louis X's. If there was more than one person with the same first name, they would add numbers to their names. For example, the 11th James to join the Nation of Islam would take the name James 11 X.

SCENE 2: April 1957. Outside the 28th Precinct police station in Harlem.

NARRATOR: With Malcolm's help the Nation of Islam began to grow, attracting young people and even many ex-convicts. Still, the organization remained "underground"—it had very little influence and was known to only a handful of people outside of poor neighborhoods in a few large cities. That changed in April of 1957, when the police in Harlem roughed up a young black man. Malcolm and other members of the Nation of Islam came to his aid.

MALCOLM: I demand to see the young man you just arrested.

POLICE CAPTAIN: Who are you?

MALCOLM: Malcolm X

POLICE CAPTAIN: Listen, Martin Z or whatever your name is, I want you to leave at once and take your goon squad with you.

MALCOLM: *(calmly)* It's Malcolm X, captain. These men are members of the Nation of Islam. It's within our constitutional rights to gather here. Once again, I demand to see that young man.

POLICE CAPTAIN: Sure, I'll take you in to see him if you send your army there home.

MALCOLM: No deal. We have reason to believe the man you arrested needs medical attention. He may need to go to a hospital. This is reasonable and right and we will stand for nothing less. Nobody moves until we get what we want.

NARRATOR: Malcolm and the Nation of Islam won the showdown. Malcolm visited the young man, who was bleeding badly, and it was arranged that he be taken to a hospital for treatment. Word on the street spread quickly. There was a powerful new organization in Harlem, one that stood up for the rights and dignity of black people. Their leader was a fiery young man named Malcolm X.

THE END

Teacher's Guide

MALCOLM X

QUOTE

I believe that it would be almost impossible to find any-where in America a black man who has lived further down in the mud of human society than I have; or a black man who has been any more ignorant than I have been; or a black man who has suffered more anguish during his life than I have. But it is only after the deep-est darkness that the greatest joy can come; it is only after slavery and prison that the sweetest appreciation of freedom can come.

BIOGRAPHY

Malcolm X was born Malcolm Little in Omaha, Nebraska, on May 19, 1925. He was one of 11 children. His father, Reverend Earl Little, was a Baptist minister and an organizer for Marcus Garvey's Universal Negro Improvement Association. Harassed as a result of the reverend's work, the Little family moved out of Omaha. Earl Little was murdered when Malcolm was only six years old.

After the eighth grade, Malcolm dropped out of school and headed to Boston. He eventually found his way to Harlem. During this time, Malcolm became involved in illegal activities. He was arrested in Boston in 1946 for burglary and was sent to prison. While in prison, Malcolm worked to educate himself. During this period, Malcolm's brother Reginald introduced him to the Nation of Islam. Upon his release from prison in 1952, Malcolm sought out Elijah Muhammad, the nation's leader, and took the name of Malcolm X.

In March of 1964, Malcolm X left the Nation of Islam. He organized his own group, the Muslim Mosque, Inc. The split with the Nation of Islam was bitter. Malcolm's wife Betty Shabazz and the couple's four daughters survived a fire bomb attack on their house on February 14, 1965. A week later, Malcolm X was gunned down at the Audobon Ballroom in Harlem. It was suspected that the Nation of Islam was involved in the assassination. Nine months after Malcolm X's death, his autobiography was published. His words seemed to speak for many northern and urban African Americans who felt distant from the civil rights struggle in the South.

READ ABOUT HIM

* *Malcolm X* by Arnold Adoff (Crowell, 1972)
* *Malcolm X: By Any Means Necessary* by Walter Dean Myers (Scholastic, 1994)
* *Malcolm X* by Jack Rummel (Chelsea House, 1989)

TALK ABOUT HIM

Malcolm's Stages: Discuss how Malcolm changed in each stage of his life. What lessons do students think he learned at the various stages? Do they believe that Malcolm became wiser as he grew older? Why or why not? Ask students to discuss ways in which they have grown. What kinds of changes do they see for themselves in the future?

Influential Friends: Some of the following people were influential in Malcolm X's life: his activist father, his friend Bimbi, and Elijah Muhammad. Who are some of the people who have had an impact on your students' lives? Engage them in a discussion about how their lives might have been different if they hadn't known these people. What kind of impact do students feel that they have on others' lives?

WRITE ABOUT HIM

The Power of Books: Books played an extremely important role in Malcolm's life. When reporters would ask Malcolm what university he had attended, he would proudly say, "Books." Have students pick books that are of special significance to them and write book reviews, giving synopses of the plots and explaining their significance. Encourage pairs of students to trade and read books, then write their own reviews of the books. Ask them to compare the two book reviews.

The Muslim Faith: In prison, Malcolm X converted to the Muslim faith. Later, he traveled to the Muslim holy city of Mecca. Let students discover more about the importance of this city to the Muslim religion. They may wish to concentrate on the city's history, the Muslim rituals and holidays that pilgrims celebrate there, or its impact in contemporary times, such as the number of Muslim pilgrims who travel to the city and where they come from.

From A to Z: One of the ways in which Malcolm educated himself was to copy all the words and definitions from A to Z out of a dictionary. Give students access to dictionaries in the classroom or send them to the library reference section. Tell them to copy down at least 10 new words and definitions. Let students use their new words in composing essays, speeches, stories, letters, journal entries, or any other forms of writing.